Didax

SKILLS
S E R I E S

ORAL
LANGUAGE

GRADES 4-5

Published with the permission of R.I.C. Publications Pty. Ltd.

Copyright © 2007 by Didax, Inc., Rowley, MA 01969. All rights reserved.

First published by R.I.C. Publications Pty. Ltd., Perth, Western Australia. Revised by Didax Educational Resources.

Printed in the United States of America.

Order Number: 2-5275
ISBN-13: 978-1-58324-257-5

A B C D E F 11 10 09 08 07

The Association of Educational Publishers

395 Main Street
Rowley, MA 01969
www.didax.com

FOREWORD

Oral Language forms an integral part of a student's education. Our main means of communicating with the world is through speaking.

Children of today generally spend hours being passively entertained by TV and computer games. Therefore, it is vital that during their time at school, students acquire skills in speaking and listening and practice them in a variety of situations.

Obtaining these skills means not only do students learn to converse more freely, but hopefully they will gain confidence in speaking so that they can communicate more effectively; for example, in giving their own point of view, giving instructions, requesting information, giving a speech, discussing topics with peers, having conversations, talking about personal experiences and telling jokes.

The books in this series are: *Oral Language – Grades 2 to 3*
Oral Language – Grades 4 to 5
Oral Language – Grades 6 to 7

CONTENTS

Oral Language, Grades 4 to 5 provides a wide range of activities to develop students' oral language skills.

Each activity consists of two pages of worksheets and one page of accompanying teacher notes.

TEACHER PAGE

A teacher page accompanies each pair of student worksheets. It provides the following information:

Title of activity

The *Objective* section states the purpose and learning outcome of the activity.

The *Activities Covered* section lists the activities the students will undertake to complete the worksheets.

The *Background Information* section has been included to enhance the teacher's understanding of the concept being taught and provide additional information.

The *Before the Lesson* section tells teachers what they need to prepare before the lesson. It also states whether the students will be working in pairs or groups, so the teacher can decide how to group the students.

The *Lesson* section suggests, in a step-by-step format, how the lesson could be taught and the worksheets used.

The *Answers* section provides answers to all worksheet activities. Some answers will vary depending on students' personal experiences, and therefore will need a teacher check.

The *Additional Activities* section can be used to further develop the objectives being taught, as consolidation or extension. Suggestions for suitable websites are sometimes included.

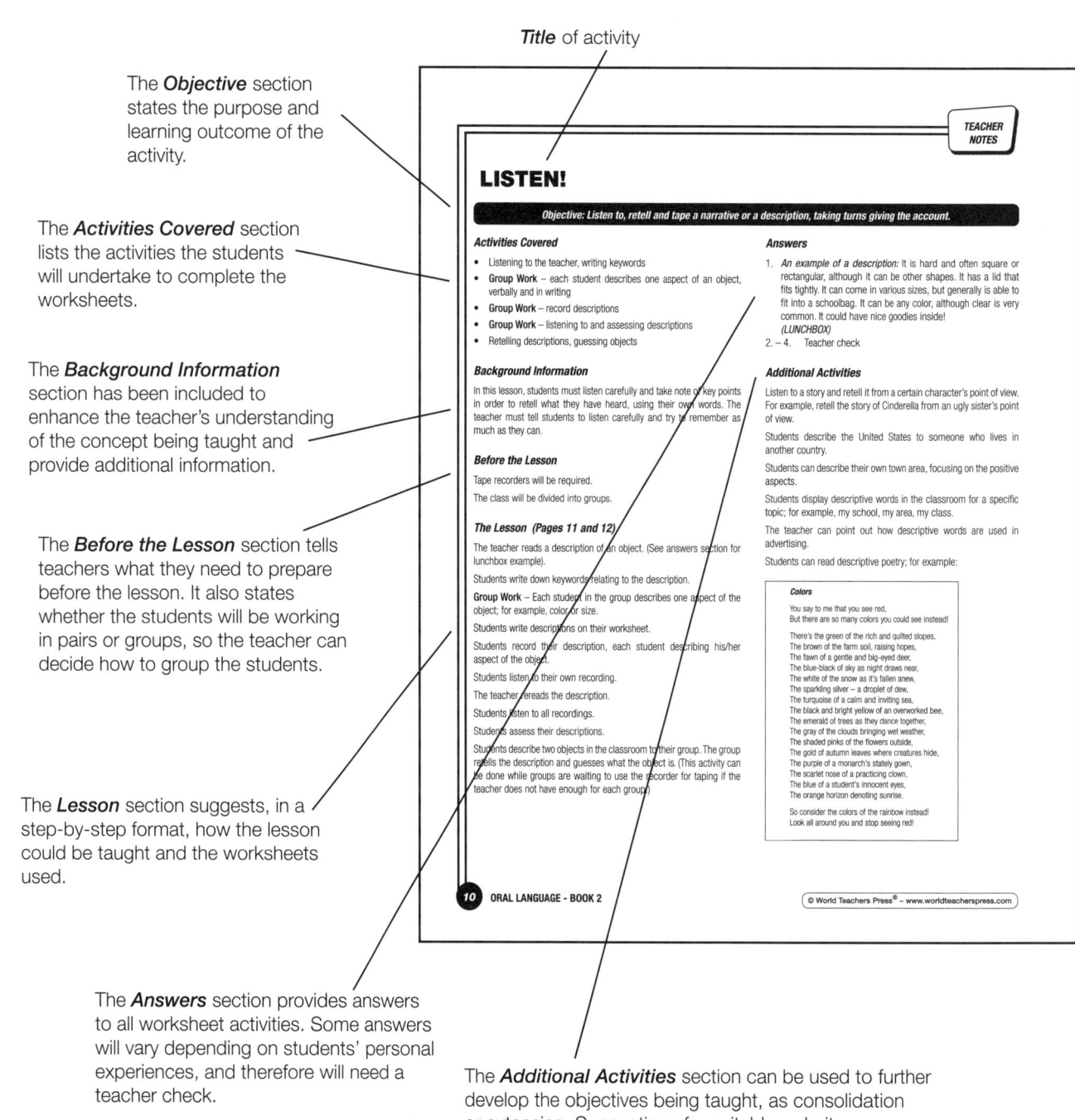

LISTEN!

Objective: Listen to, retell and tape a narrative or a description, taking turns giving the account.

Activities Covered

- Listening to the teacher, writing keywords
- **Group Work** – each student describes one aspect of an object, verbally and in writing
- **Group Work** – record descriptions
- **Group Work** – listening to and assessing descriptions
- Retelling descriptions, guessing objects

Background Information

In this lesson, students must listen carefully and take note of key points in order to retell what they have heard, using their own words. The teacher must tell students to listen carefully and try to remember as much as they can.

Before the Lesson

Tape recorders will be required.

The class will be divided into groups.

The Lesson (Pages 11 and 12)

The teacher reads a description of an object. (See answers section for lunchbox example).

Students write down keywords relating to the description.

Group Work – Each student in the group describes one aspect of the object; for example, color or size.

Students write descriptions on their worksheet.

Students record their description, each student describing his/her aspect of the object.

Students listen to their own recording.

The teacher rereads the description.

Students listen to all recordings.

Students assess their descriptions.

Students describe two objects in the classroom to their group. The group retells the description and guesses what the object is. (This activity can be done while groups are waiting to use the recorder for taping if the teacher does not have enough for each group.)

Answers

1. *An example of a description:* It is hard and often square or rectangular, although it can be other shapes. It has a lid that fits tightly. It can come in various sizes, but generally is able to fit into a schoolbag. It can be any color, although clear is very common. It could have nice goodies inside! *(LUNCHBOX)*
2. – 4.   Teacher check

Additional Activities

Listen to a story and retell it from a certain character's point of view. For example, retell the story of Cinderella from an ugly sister's point of view.

Students describe the United States to someone who lives in another country.

Students can describe their own town area, focusing on the positive aspects.

Students display descriptive words in the classroom for a specific topic; for example, my school, my area, my class.

The teacher can point out how descriptive words are used in advertising.

Students can read descriptive poetry; for example:

> *Colors*
>
> You say to me that you see red,
> But there are so many colors you could see instead!
>
> There's the green of the rich and quilted slopes,
> The brown of the farm soil, raising hopes,
> The fawn of a gentle and big-eyed deer,
> The blue-black of sky as night draws near,
> The white of the snow as it's fallen anew,
> The sparkling silver – a droplet of dew,
> The turquoise of a calm and inviting sea,
> The black and bright yellow of an overworked bee,
> The emerald of trees as they dance together,
> The gray of the clouds bringing wet weather,
> The shaded pinks of the flowers outside,
> The gold of autumn leaves where creatures hide,
> The purple of a monarch's stately gown,
> The scarlet nose of a practicing clown,
> The blue of a student's innocent eyes,
> The orange horizon denoting sunrise.
>
> So consider the colors of the rainbow instead!
> Look all around you and stop seeing red!

10   ORAL LANGUAGE – BOOK 2

© World Teachers Press® ~ www.worldteacherspress.com

STUDENT'S WORKSHEETS

Each page of teacher notes is followed by two worksheets for students to complete. A variety of worksheets are provided, which may require students to read, discuss, answer questions, write, draw, record thoughts or opinions, follow instructions, etc.

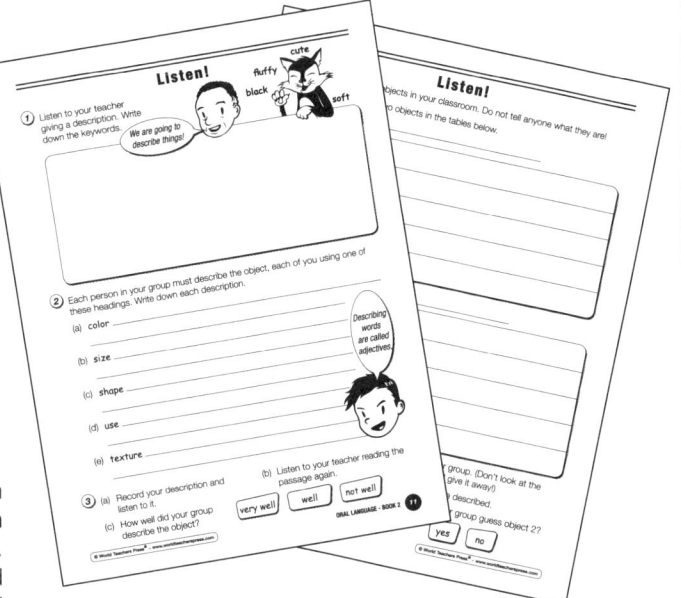

ADDITIONAL TEACHER INFORMATION

There is a great deal of group work, pair work and class work in these lessons. Teachers should not feel daunted by this. Even though it is an oral language lesson, there must be structure to it. Guidelines need to be given to students as to what they can and cannot do. During group work and pair work, teachers should walk around, assisting where necessary. If a teacher thinks it is necessary, a group leader can be appointed. Change these positions from time to time. Students should be moved around in pairs or in groups so they get to communicate with students they have not had much contact with. Teachers can explain to students that this will happen from time to time and students should not show dissatisfaction when placed with others—there will be times when they can be with their friends. The teacher should decide who will make up the pairs/groups before the lesson begins.

Some allowance has to be made for less able students or students who are extremely shy. The teacher should, in such cases, be encouraging and try to involve the student in the activity. There are also students who are very confident about speaking out loud, and such students could dominate activities. This should be gently discouraged!

The teacher is obviously the best person to set the example of how we should communicate orally. Teachers should, in most cases, correct students when they use slang or an incorrect word, but the teacher should always approach this in a friendly and sensitive manner.

As the lessons are photocopiable, a suggestion is that all talking and listening worksheets be kept in a folder, or students could have their own "oral language portfolio." Then, at the end of the year, it can be clearly seen what oral language has been covered and there won't be worksheets lying all over the place.

A few websites have been included. Although these have been checked, the teacher should check again before using them. There is a large number of great websites that would enhance many of these lessons, and teachers should make use of them with their students.

Interesting facts are also included on many of the worksheets.

Suggestions for poetry, mostly humorous poetry, have been provided. Obviously, poetry is not always funny, but at this level we don't want students becoming afraid of poetry. Rather, we want them enjoying and understanding it. Teachers must use their discretion about extra reading for the lessons, and use whatever they think will best suit their class.

Some teachers may feel a little uneasy about teaching oral language as it is a lesson of talking, something we are always telling students not to do! The teacher has the ability to set the correct tone for the lesson, and provided guidelines have been explained to the students, there should be no problems. If lessons are going to be particularly noisy, there is no harm in taking the lesson to the playground, if the weather permits! Oral language lessons should be lessons that both the teacher and students look forward to.

Have fun!

Oral Language Assessment Form

Name

Class

Date

Curriculum strand

Curriculum objective

Task(s)

The student was asked to:

Assessment

The student:	Demonstrated	Needs further opportunity

Teacher comment

HARDER WORDS

Objective: Experience the teacher's use of challenging vocabulary and structure.

Activities Covered

- Listening to the teacher
- Guessing the meaning of words
- Discussing answers with the class
- **Group Work** – writing sentences using new vocabulary
- Looking up words in the dictionary
- Using new words orally

Background Information

Students should be encouraged to ask questions in class when they do not understand new vocabulary. This should be an ongoing process. Students should write new vocabulary and meanings in their own wordbook or spelling journal. Students should be encouraged to listen to how the teacher speaks.

Before the Lesson

The teacher can have more examples of challenging words (used in context) not used in this lesson.

The class will be divided into groups and then in pairs.

The Lesson (Pages 4 and 5)

The teacher reads a sentence and students must guess the meaning of the word on their worksheet (see answer section for sentence ideas).

These questions should be read one by one, with time given after each reading of a sentence for students to work out the meaning.

Students discuss their answers with the class and check the correct meaning. At this point, teachers can read the sentence again.

Group Work – Students write three sentences using the new vocabulary.

Students read their sentences to the class.

Students guess the meanings of a list of words and then look up the meanings in a dictionary.

Students use all of the new vocabulary in oral sentences.

Answers

1. (a) an angry look (b) broken down (c) catch
   (d) danger   (e) shy   (f) deadly
   (g) large   (h) hardly ever (i) prank
   (j) annoy   (k) rough   (l) on time

2. Teacher check

3. Ideas for sentences:
   (a) Please don't *glare* at me like that; I've done nothing wrong!
   (b) This *ramshackle* house will have to be knocked down and built from scratch.
   (c) The police think they will *capture* the thief soon.
   (d) You will be in *peril* if you try to climb that high wall.
   (e) The *timid* pupil was afraid to stand up and give a talk.
   (f) Medicine can be *lethal* if not taken as instructed by the doctor.
   (g) My backpack was too *bulky* to carry up the mountain.
   (h) We are so good we *seldom* get sent to the principal's office.
   (i) There was a bomb scare in town, but it was a *hoax.*
   (j) You should not *vex* your teacher early in the morning.
   (k) The fabric of this sweater is so *coarse* it is scratching my skin.
   (l) You should get up early and be *punctual* for school.

4. Teacher check

5. (a) *scarce* – rare, few, uncommon, unusual
   (b) *remove* – take away, get rid of, throw away, take off, expel, take out
   (c) *mirth* – laughter, merriment
   (d) *tremble* – shake, quiver
   (e) *hefty* – heavy, bulky, muscular
   (f) *conceal* – hide, cover up, disguise
   (g) *placard* – poster, notice

6. Teacher check

7. (a) a nickname   (b) Yes – A bantling is a young child!

Additional Activities

Students listen to the teacher describing familiar things. Students must decipher what the words mean and replace them with a word of similar meaning; for example: The fun ride was *exhilarating*./The students were very *obedient* and the teacher was proud of them.

Students can display difficult words and their meanings in the classroom and be encouraged to use new vocabulary in their writing.

Students can read challenging poetry.

The teacher can give the students a challenging passage using all new words that have been learned and students can write it in the language they know. This activity can also be done the other way around.

Harder Words

1 Listen to the teacher and circle what you think these words mean.

In this lesson we are going to learn harder words. Try to use them in your conversations.

(a) glare–
an angry look
shine
swear

(b) ramshackle–
beautiful
broken down
large

(c) capture–
hug
catch
shoot

(d) peril–
love
trouble
danger

(e) timid–
shy
tiny
naughty

(f) lethal–
expensive
helpful
deadly

(g) bulky–
empty
large
colorful

(h) seldom–
hardly ever
always
never

(i) hoax–
prank
object
plan

(j) vex–
insult
help
annoy

(k) coarse–
fluffy
rough
cheap

(l) punctual–
on time
neat
quiet

2 Discuss your answers with your class and check the correct answers! How many did you get correct?

You should listen to the way your teacher speaks!

3 Work as a group to choose three of the words above and use them in sentences of your own.

(a) _____

_____

(b) _____

_____

(c) _____

_____

4 Read your sentences to the class.

Harder Words

(5)

Word	Your Meaning	Dictionary Meaning
(a) scarce		
(b) remove		
(c) mirth		
(d) tremble		
(e) hefty		
(f) conceal		
(g) placard		

(6) Work with a partner to use each of the words in Question 5 in an oral sentence.

We used ☐ out of 7 words in oral sentences.

(7) (a)

Can you guess what a moniker is?

(b)

Is this child a bantling?

LISTEN!

Objective: Listen to, retell and tape a narrative or a description, taking turns giving the account.

Activities Covered

- Listening to the teacher, writing keywords
- **Group Work** – each student describes one aspect of an object, verbally and in writing
- **Group Work** – record descriptions
- **Group Work** – listening to and assessing descriptions
- Retelling descriptions, guessing objects

Background Information

In this lesson, students must listen carefully and take note of key points in order to retell what they have heard, using their own words. The teacher must tell students to listen carefully and try to remember as much as they can.

Before the Lesson

Tape recorders will be required.

The class will be divided into groups.

The Lesson (Pages 11 and 12)

The teacher reads a description of an object. (See answers section for lunchbox example).

Students write down keywords relating to the description.

Group Work – Each student in the group describes one aspect of the object; for example, color or size.

Students write descriptions on their worksheet.

Students record their description, each student describing his/her aspect of the object.

Students listen to their own recording.

The teacher rereads the description.

Students listen to all recordings.

Students assess their descriptions.

Students describe two objects in the classroom to their group. The group retells the description and guesses what the object is. (This activity can be done while groups are waiting to use the recorder for taping if the teacher does not have enough for each group.)

Answers

1. *An example of a description:* It is hard and often square or rectangular, although it can be other shapes. It has a lid that fits tightly. It can come in various sizes, but generally is able to fit into a schoolbag. It can be any color, although clear is very common. It could have nice goodies inside!
(LUNCHBOX)
2.–4.   Teacher check

Additional Activities

Listen to a story and retell it from a certain character's point of view. For example, retell the story of Cinderella from an ugly sister's point of view.

Students describe the United States to someone who lives in another country.

Students can describe their own town area, focusing on the positive aspects.

Students display descriptive words in the classroom for a specific topic; for example, my school, my area, my class.

The teacher can point out how descriptive words are used in advertising.

Students can read descriptive poetry; for example:

Colors

You say to me that you see red,
But there are so many colors you could see instead!

There's the green of the rich and quilted slopes,
The brown of the farm soil, raising hopes,
The fawn of a gentle and big-eyed deer,
The blue-black of sky as night draws near,
The white of the snow as it's fallen anew,
The sparkling silver – a droplet of dew,
The turquoise of a calm and inviting sea,
The black and bright yellow of an overworked bee,
The emerald of trees as they dance together,
The gray of the clouds bringing wet weather,
The shaded pinks of the flowers outside,
The gold of autumn leaves where creatures hide,
The purple of a monarch's stately gown,
The scarlet nose of a practicing clown,
The blue of a student's innocent eyes,
The orange horizon denoting sunrise.

So consider the colors of the rainbow instead!
Look all around you and stop seeing red!

Listen!

1 Listen to your teacher giving a description. Write down the keywords.

We are going to describe things!

cute
fluffy
black
soft

2 Each person in your group must describe the object, each of you using one of these headings. Write down each description.

(a) **color** _____

_____

(b) **size** _____

_____

(c) **shape** _____

_____

Describing words are called adjectives.

(d) **use** _____

_____

(e) **texture** _____

_____

3 (a) Record your description and listen to it.

(b) Listen to your teacher reading the passage again.

(c) How well did your group describe the object?

very well   well   not well

Listen!

④ (a) Choose two objects in your classroom. Do not tell anyone what they are!

(b) Describe the two objects in the tables below.

Object 1 is _____

color	
size	
shape	
use	
texture	

Object 2 is _____

color	
size	
shape	
use	
texture	

(c) Use your notes to retell your descriptions to your group. (Don't look at the object when you are describing it, or else you will give it away!)

(d) Your group needs to guess which objects you have described.

• Did your group guess object 1?

yes   no

• Did your group guess object 2?

yes   no

FOLLOW THE INSTRUCTIONS!

Objective: Give and follow instructions on how to perform a particular task or process.

Activities Covered

- Drawing pictures for instructions
- Writing instructions to go with pictures
- **Pair Work** – giving clues (directions) to find pictures

Background Information

In this lesson, students are working with giving instructions and directions. The class can discuss when in life we follow instructions and directions; for example, reading a map, reading a recipe, building a model, reading road signs, etc.

Before the Lesson

The teacher can bring to school various food labels/items that have cooking instructions on them for students to look at.

The teacher could show students a saucepan, salt, pasta, a wooden spoon and some pasta sauce to help them draw their answers to Question 1.

The class will be divided into pairs.

The Lesson (Pages 14 and 15)

Students draw pictures on their worksheet to go with the instructions for cooking pasta.

Students write instructions for given pictures, showing how to wash your hands.

Pair Work – Students decide where the treasure is buried and must give verbal directions to their partner on how to find it.

Answers

1. Teacher check
2. Answers could vary, but could include:
   Turn on the faucet.
   Wet your hands.
   Rub soap on your hands to wash them.
   Turn off the faucet.
   Dry your hands.
3–4. Teacher check

Additional Activities

Students can write instructions for the petsitter on how to take care of their pet.

Students can write instructions on how to be good in class!

Students can bring from home food labels/packaging where instructions are given. These can be displayed in the classroom.

Students can do simple crafts following simple given instructions.

Students can read different recipes and follow them to make some delicious snacks.

Students assemble objects/toys—for example, Lego® models—with one student giving directions and the other building.

Follow the Instructions!

1 Draw a series of pictures to go with these instructions.

(a)

Bring a large pan of slightly salted water to a boil.

(b)

Add the pasta and bring back to a boil.

(c)

Boil for about ten minutes, stirring every now and then.

(d)

Drain well.

(e)

Serve tossed in sauce.

2 Write instructions to go with these pictures.

(a)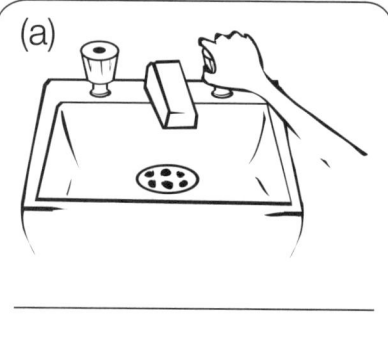

_____

_____

(b)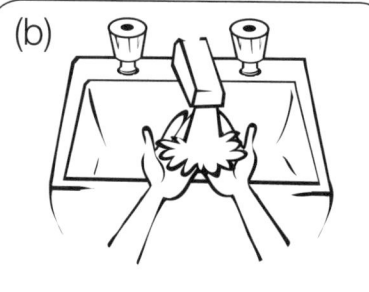

_____

_____

(c)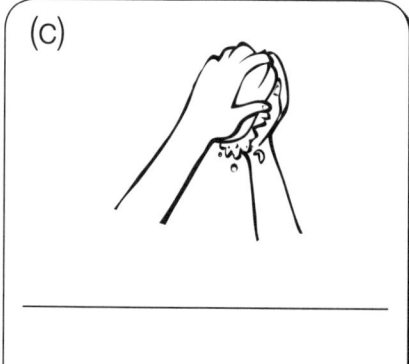

_____

_____

(d)

_____

_____

(e)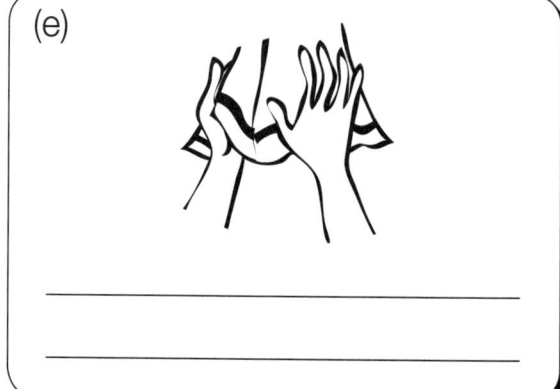

_____

_____

3 Discuss your answers with your teacher.

Follow the Instructions!

4 (a) Look at this treasure map. Decide where the treasure is buried and give your partner clues on how to find it. Make him or her go through a series of steps to get there, starting at the sailing ship.

Did you know? The magnetic compass is a Chinese invention (about 221–206 B.C.).

(b) When you have finished, mark the buried treasure using an "X."

(c) Did your partner find the treasure? | yes | | no |

(d) Were your instructions easy to follow? | yes | | sometimes | | no |

SPEAK UP!

Objective: Become increasingly aware of the importance of voice, audibility and clarity of enunciation in communicating with others.

Activities Covered

- Listening to teacher – writing words
- **Pair Work** – reading poem, first mumbling, then speaking clearly

Background Information

This lesson focuses on speaking clearly and pronouncing words properly. This is an ongoing process throughout the year; this lesson just shows students how speaking clearly can make a big difference. The teacher should explain that if we want others to listen to us, they must be able to understand us!

Before the Lesson

The teacher can have a passage/poem/short story which will be read to the class. (See Answers section for an example.)

The teacher can practice reading something by mumbling.

The class will be divided into pairs.

The Lesson (Pages 17 and 18)

The teacher reads a passage/poem/short story in a mumble.

Students write down any keywords they heard.

The teacher reads the passage again, this time speaking clearly and pronouncing the words properly.

Students again write down any keywords they heard.

The teacher can discuss with the class the difference between the two readings.

Pair Work – Students read the given poem in a mumble, then reread it clearly, pronouncing all the words correctly. Some pairs can read the poem to the class.

Answers

1.–5.   Teacher check

An example of a reading that can be read to the class:

> **Hungry**
>
> Mom, I'm almost withering away,
> I've had almost nothing to eat today!
> Why for breakfast, I munched an orange on toast,
> And leftover egg with Sunday roast.
> I slurped pea soup and a cup of tea,
> That isn't enough, I know you'd agree!
> For lunch, all I had was spinach pie,
> And chopped up liver on moldy rye.
> I picked six wormy apples from the apple tree,
> Why I'm so famished, you can clearly see!
> Then for dinner, I nibbled on six lamb chops,
> With pigs' feet, brussels and corn pops.
> Then bread and cheese mixed with ham,
> And two jars of outdated jam.
> So, Mom, quick, bring me food on a tray!
> I've had almost nothing to eat today!

Additional Activities

Students role-play talking clearly and appropriately to different people; for example, a friend's parents, the Queen of England, the President, an uncle, etc.

Students listen to and copy different accents.

Speak Up!

When we speak, others must be able to hear what we are saying.

You should always speak clearly!

1 (a) Listen to your teacher. Write down any words that you heard.

_____

_____

_____

_____

(b) How many words did you write? _____

2 (a) Listen to your teacher again. Write down keywords that you heard this time.

_____

_____

_____

_____

_____

_____

(b) How many words did you write? _____

3 (a) Which reading did you hear the most words for?

1st reading	2nd reading

(b) Why? _____

_____

Speak Up!

4 Pair work:

(a) Read this poem to each other, first mumbling it, then saying it very clearly together.

*Did you know?
A tribe of people called the San people talk only with a series of clicks!*

12 O'Clock Feeding

*We tiptoed quietly down the wooden stairs,
clutching our favorite teddy bears.
Our tummies were rumbling, we needed to eat,
we sneaked to the kitchen in slippered feet.
We took out chips and bread and jam,
as well as cheese and honeyed ham.
We found some nuts and a piece of cake,
leftover chips and garlic steak.
It wasn't enough, we needed more,
we pulled out sausages from the freezer drawer.
We fried them quickly in a pan,
and dished out baked beans from a can.
Then there we sat with our mountain of food,
I wasn't sure now if we were quite in the mood.
All of this bustling had made us quite tired,
there was a sleepiness we'd all acquired.
We nibbled a little, our appetites ceased.
The Sandman had ruined our midnight feast.*

(b) Which reading sounded better?   Mumbled / Clear

5 Write the words that were the most difficult to pronounce properly.

_____

_____

_____

_____

NO WORDS!

Objective: Use mime to convey ideas, reactions, emotions, desires and attitudes.

Activities Covered

- Writing and drawing a wish and a job
- Miming a wish and a job
- **Pair Work** – writing conversation
- Miming conversation
- Self-assessment

Background Information

Mime should already have been introduced at a younger age, but the teacher can recap what has been learned. The teacher must explain to the class that actions need to be exaggerated in order to get their message across.

Before the Lesson

The class will be divided into groups of about six students and then into pairs.

The Lesson (Pages 20 and 21)

The teacher can briefly discuss what mime is and how it should be done.

Students write and draw on their sheet a wish that they have and a job they would like to do.

Students mime this wish and job to their group, who must try to guess what they are.

Students write if the group guessed correctly.

Pair Work – Students write down a conversation between an angry teacher and a student.

In pairs, students practice this conversation, using mime only.

A few of the pairs can present their mime to the class if there is time.

Answers

1.–2.   Teacher check
3.   Answers will vary, but an example is:
        Teacher: Why on earth is this homework not done?
        Student: Well, Mrs. Brown, there was a fierce wind last night ...
        Teacher: I don't care about the weather, boy! Where is your work?
        Student: But Mrs. Brown, the wind took our roof off!
        Teacher: Why did you need a roof to complete your work?
        Student: Well, Mrs. Brown, I did my work, but without a roof, the rain ruined it!
4.–5.   Teacher check

Additional Activities

Students can have conversations using mime only.

Discuss the history of mime. Teachers can get some information on this website: *www.mime.info*

Students can use mime in other subjects; for example, to show different stories from history.

Students can mime poetry. For example:

Wishing Well

If I could be granted a wish,
I think that it would be,
To have a giant trampoline,
Just for my friends and me.

I'd have a sparkling swimming pool,
And a leopard as a pet.
I think I'd own an ice cream shop,
And my very own Lear jet.

I'd have a gigantic bedroom,
Stuffed with games and toys,
A designer wooden treehouse,
With a plaque saying 'Only boys!'

I'd have a pantry packed with chocolate,
And my own designer cook,
Who specialized in pizza,
And had written his own book.

I think I'd have a playground,
And my very own football club.
I'd be chauffeured in my limo,
Complete with loo and tub.

I'd have the latest Playstation™,
And a hundred-foot TV.
And as for quads and go-karts,
Why, I'd have more than three!

But, oops, I'm getting carried away.
One wish is not enough!
I need a bunch of genies
To order all this stuff.

No Words!

To mime means to act without words. Your actions will have to show what you are trying to say.

(1) Think of something you really wish for.

(a) What is it? _____

(b) Draw it below.

Did you know?
The first known mime was performed in 467 B.C.

(c) Mime it for your group.

(d) Did your group guess what your wish is? _____

No talking!

(2) Think of a job you would like to do when you are an adult.

(a) What is it? _____

(b) Draw it below.

(c) Mime it for your group.

(d) Did your group guess what your chosen job is? _____

No Words!

3 Work with a partner to write a conversation between an angry teacher and a student.

Some ideas are:

Student has not done homework.

Student has taken another student's pen.

Student has forgotten his/her gym uniform.

Student has been talking during assembly.

Teacher: _____

_____

Student: _____

_____

Teacher: _____

_____

Student: _____

_____

Teacher: _____

_____

Student: _____

_____

Teacher: _____

_____

Student: _____

_____

4 Now try to mime it!

5 Color the stars to assess your mime.

SOUND IT OUT!

Objective: *Discuss the use and effect of music, sound effects and nonverbal clues in audio tapes, videotapes and film clips.*

Activities Covered

- Listening to and watching TV excerpt
- Answering questions
- Discussing answers to questions
- **Group Work –** presenting a reading of a poem using sound effects

Background Information

Students will often sit mesmerized in front of the TV screen, totally unaware of all the tactics used to entice them and hold their attention. This lesson focuses on one aspect—sound. The idea is not to put students off watching TV (as if!), but rather to make them aware of the different components. Other lessons can focus on color, special effects, acting, etc.

Before the Lesson

The teacher must have a TV excerpt where sound effects and music are used. This can be part of a program, movie, or advertisement.

The Lesson (Pages 23 and 24)

The teacher can briefly discuss how music and sound effects are used in films, programs, advertisements, etc.

Students watch the TV excerpt the teacher has chosen.

Students answer questions about the TV excerpt.

Students discuss all their answers with the class.

Group Work – Students read a poem and add sound effects.

Students present their poem to the class.

Students discuss which would be more effective: a poem with or without sound effects.

Answers

Teacher check

Additional Activities

For homework, students can watch TV and take note of sound effects and music used, writing brief notes. Students must then report their findings to the class.

Students can be given the particulars of a product, and they must then make up a jingle for it.

Students can read sound poems and bring items from home to make sound effects suitable for the poem. This could be done in groups.

Sound It Out!

Do you notice the music and sound effects when you watch TV?

1 Watch the TV excerpt the teacher shows you and answer these questions.

(a) What did you watch?

_____

_____

(c) What effect did they have?

_____

_____

_____

_____

_____

(e) How did the music help?

_____

_____

(b) What sound effects were used?

_____

_____

_____

_____

_____

(d) What kind of music was used?

_____

_____

_____

_____

2 Can you think of a jingle used on TV? What does the jingle advertise?

_____

3 Why do advertisements make use of sound effects and music? _____

_____

_____

4 Discuss your answers with the class.

Be aware of sounds and music when you are watching TV!

Sound It Out!

⑤ Work as a group to practice and perform this "noisy" poem to your class.

Make sure that every member of your group:

(a) reads part of the poem

(b) makes at least one of the sound effects

(c) writes on the poem what he/she has to do.

Silence Is Not Golden

*The house is crowded with
shattering, crackling, shrieking
sounds of
students running, talking,
whispering, shouting, calling.
"Bang!" goes the door,
feet on the wooden floor.
Plates are rattling and glasses
tinkling,
water running, cutlery clanging,
music blaring, TV chatting,
drawers are squeaking and
skateboards scraping.
Soon the windows will shatter
with the fullness of it.
The noise will go spilling out
onto the street.
And the house will be quiet,
and the comfort,
gone.*

PICTURE THIS!

Objective: Understand the relationship between text and illustration.

Activities Covered

- Listening to teacher, drawing picture
- Matching pictures and sentences
- **Pair Work** – writing sentences that suit the picture and reading them aloud to the class

Background Information

This lesson makes students aware of the association between text and pictures. Students must come to notice that pictures in stories, poems, articles, etc., often relate to the words and can give us more information. The teacher should bring examples to class of how pictures enhance the text.

Before the Lesson

The teacher can have ready a passage that can be read to the class which the students must draw. (See below for an example.)

The teacher should have a few examples of where illustrations have been used; for example, in poetry books, photos in the newspaper, advertising leaflets, fairy tales, recipes, instructions.

The class will be divided into pairs.

The Lesson (Pages 26 and 27)

Students listen to the teacher telling a story/reading passage/reading a poem and draw a picture to go with it.

Students match pictures and sentences.

Pair Work – Students discuss and write sentences to go with given pictures.

Students read out Question 3 sentences to the class.

Students draw pictures to match the sentences.

Answers

1.–4. Teacher check
    Example of a passage that can be read to the class:

James and Marie couldn't wait to get to the zoo. It was a freezing cold day but they didn't notice. James had seen elephants on TV and had read hundreds of books about them, but he had never actually seen them with his own eyes. Marie, on the other hand, was mad about reptiles. While her friends went into a frenzy when they saw pictures of snakes, Marie was fascinated. Once they got through the zoo gates, there was no stopping them. James found the elephants and just stood there and stared at them. He said he was in heaven. Marie ran from one reptile cage to another; there were so many snakes and lizards to see.

James and Marie reluctantly looked at a few other animals, but spent most of their day observing the creatures they had dreamed about. They were the last to leave the zoo, and the gate had even been locked! Their parents had to almost drag them away with a promise that they would visit once a month.

Many years later, James became a game ranger in a South African wildlife reserve, elephants being among the animals under his care. Marie worked in a snake park in Australia. The pair of them write the most fascinating emails to each other about their various adventures with the creatures they love.

Additional Activities

Students can match photos and captions.

Students can bring photos from home and add a caption. These can all be displayed in the classroom.

Students can draw pictures to go with a poem; for example:

Elementary Zoo

Our classroom is just like the zoo,
with creatures tame and wild,
some with habits peculiar,
and some with manners mild.

There are the colorful parrots,
and all they do is yak,
and then we have some lemmings,
it's sense that they do lack.

There's those that strut about like lions,
kings of the jungle are they,
and hairy big orangutans,
that simply want to play.

We also have a variety of snakes,
of the venomous sort,
and an array of spindly spiders,
in whose web you might get caught.

We have some snobby, snooty cats,
their noses stuck in the air,
and prickly, stickly echidnas,
of them you must beware!

Gratefully, there are gentle lambs,
who never hurt or shout,
and quiet, squeaky little mice,
who live in fear, no doubt!

Yes, our room is full and noisy,
with beasts of every kind.
The zookeeper, Miss Krout, says,
We drive her out of her mind!

Picture This!

1 Listen to your teacher. Draw a picture to go with what the teacher has read.

2 Draw a picture to illustrate each sentence.

Pictures can give us more information!

(a) It would be great if Jenny were here now. •••••

(b) He yells at us for doing that! •••••

(c) Everyone should have a hobby that helps them to relax. •••••

Picture This!

3 Work with a partner to write sentences to go with these pictures.
Read your sentences out to the class.

(a)

_____
_____
_____

(b)

_____
_____
_____

(c)

_____
_____
_____

4 Draw pictures to illustrate these sentences.

(a) Sue and Abdul were best friends.

(b) The police officer chased the robber.

WHAT IS YOUR OPINION?

Objective: Give and take turns in speaking and experience a classroom environment in which tolerance for the views of others is fostered.

Activities Covered

- Writing down opinions
- Responding to comments
- Reading text, giving own opinion
- Discussing all answers with the class
- Surveying opinions

Background Information

When any type of oral language takes place in the classroom, students must be encouraged to take turns in speaking, as well as to respect and accept the views of others. It is important that students are told to always speak one at a time and not to criticize the opinions of others. Teachers should explain to students that they do not have to agree with others, but should be tolerant of others' ideas.

Before the Lesson

The teacher should have ready points for discussion as to how we can accept the views of others.

The teacher should introduce various outrageous/unpopular views to get students used to accepting different views. For example, visit the website of The Flat Earth Society
www.alaska.net/~clund/e_djublonskopf/Flatearthsociety.htm

The Lesson (Pages 29 and 30)

Have a class discussion about different views and how we can accept the opinions and ideas of others.

Students write their opinions on various different things.

Students respond to statements, not necessarily agreeing with but accepting the views of others.

Students read the text and comment on Jim and Carla's views.

All answers should be discussed with the class and opinions surveyed.

Answers

1. Teacher check
2. Answers will vary, but could include:
   (a) "I like broccoli with cheese."/"Broccoli is not my favorite vegetable."
   (b) "I seem to take hours to do my homework every day."/"I would not like more homework because then I would have no time to play."/"I love doing homework, so I wouldn't mind getting more."
3.–4. Teacher check

Additional Activities

Students can make up ridiculous statements to tell the class, who should try not to ridicule or laugh! For example, they might say "My grandmother is a secret spy!"

Students can give their opinions about a particular topic from another subject—for example, nutrition in science—and these opinions can be displayed in the classroom.

Students can read the following poem and discuss the opinions of the different family members.

Almost a Family Affair

Now on Sundays, our family sits down to a feast,
of an assortment of veggies and carved-up roast beast.
Jamie loves potatoes all covered in sauce,
Josh likes the trifle, with ice cream of course!
Jason wants gravy all over his plate,
and beef puts Dad in an excitable state.
Luke adores peas, though we can't think of why,
and Shaun, warm rolls, eaten just dry.
Spot chews the bone once we're all done,
and Fluffy eats scraps, leaving us none.
Yes, we all have a favorite part of the meal,
although Mom seems to get a slightly raw deal.
I don't think roast dinner's Mom's first choice of food,
because she doesn't each much and seems in a mood!
She gets even worse when it's time to clear away,
You'd swear she didn't enjoy being in the kitchen all day!

What Is Your Opinion?

We all have our own opinions on things. Some of us may love science, while others prefer math!

Always respect others' views, even though they may not be the same as yours.

1 What is your opinion of the following?

(a) pizza _____

(b) trampolines _____

(c) math _____

(d) milk _____

(e) dinosaurs _____

(f) soccer _____

(g) the color pink _____

(h) brussels sprouts _____

(i) classical music _____

(j) newspapers _____

2 Respond to these statements. You don't have to agree, but respect the views.

(a) The best thing to have on bread is broccoli.

_____
_____
_____

(b) I wish we could get extra homework.

_____
_____
_____

What Is Your Opinion?

3 Read Jim's view of school.

> School is the best place for a kid to be. As well as talking to and seeing all our friends, we also get to learn about the world around us. If I didn't go to school, I would get so bored. Why do we have weekends?

(a) Do you agree or disagree with Jim? _____

(b) Why? _____

_____

_____

(c) How many people in your class:

- agree with Jim? ☐
- disagree with Jim? ☐

4 Read Carla's view of the Harry Potter books.

> I love reading the Harry Potter books! They are so exciting, and you never know what is going to happen to Harry, Ron and Hermione next. The lessons at Hogwarts sound really interesting and quidditch looks fun.

(a) Do you agree or disagree with Carla?

_____

(b) Why? _____

_____

_____

_____

_____

_____

_____

_____

(c) How many people in your class:

- agree with Carla? ☐
- disagree with Carla? ☐

TALK ABOUT IT!

Objective: Initiate conversations and respond to the initiatives of others in talking about experiences and activities.

Activities Covered

- Writing about experiences
- Telling about an experience
- Asking and answering questions about an experience
- Responding to comments
- **Pair Work –** Having conversation

Background Information

This lesson gets students to have a conversation on things they have personally experienced. Students first think about and write down their experiences before they discuss them. The teacher can give students practice in conversation by presenting a topic to start with, which they must keep going. This can be done whenever there is spare time, and the students won't mind!

Before the Lesson

The teacher can have examples of good and bad experiences; perhaps newspaper cuttings can be used.

The class will be divided into groups of four or five students and then pairs.

The Lesson (Pages 32 and 33)

Have a class discussion on experiences and allow students to give their own, short account of an experience they have had.

The teacher can go through the questions on the sheet so that students know what is expected of them.

Students write down experiences they have had.

Group Work – Students take it in turns to tell about an experience they have had. The other members of the group ask questions about the experience, which the student has to answer.

Students respond to comments using speech balloons. Encourage students to answer the questions with another question, as this technique would keep the conversation going for longer.

Pair Work – Students use the ideas from Questions 1–3 to start conversations and keep them going.

Give students a time limit for their conversation and tell them to try to keep it going!

Answers

1.–2.   Teacher check
3.   Answers will vary, but could include:
   (a) Did you not enjoy your last birthday?/What happened to you on your last birthday?
   (b) Yes, all this rain means we're stuck indoors. When was the last time we had sunshine?
   (c) Me too! Are you doing anything special?
   (d) Why are you so hungry; didn't you have any breakfast?/ What would you like for lunch?
4.   Teacher check

Additional Activities

In pairs, students can talk about their experience of sports; for example, "My experience of sports is watching football on TV. I have never been able to play myself but I wish that I could." or, "My experience of sports is playing tennis twice a week for our local club. I love the sport, and I hope to be at Wimbledon one day."

Talk About It!

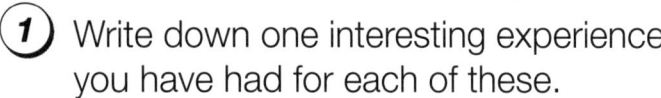

Everyone has had some sort of experience. You're having one right now. I hope it's not a boring one!

They're not having a great experience!

1 Write down one interesting experience you have had for each of these.

(a) Shopping _____

_____
_____
_____
_____

(b) A farm/zoo/park _____

_____
_____
_____
_____

(c) A holiday _____

_____
_____
_____
_____

(d) Visiting a relative _____

_____
_____
_____
_____

2 (a) Choose one of your experiences.

The experience I have chosen is _____

(b) Tell your group about your experience.

How well do you think you told your group?

| really well / | quite well / | OK / | not very well / |

(c) Your group will ask you questions about your experience.

How many questions could you answer?  out of

Talk About It!

3 Write down something you could say to keep each conversation going.

(a) I really hope this birthday is better than my last!

_____
_____
_____

(b) I wish this weather would improve!

_____
_____
_____

(c) I am really looking forward to school vacation!

_____
_____
_____

(d) I hope there's something nice for lunch. I'm starving!

_____
_____
_____

Don't stop talking!

4 Practice conversations with a partner. Use ideas from Questions 1, 2 and 3 to start your conversation. Try to keep talking! (This is something you won't often hear your teacher say!)

Rate your conversation (A is excellent).

| A | B | C | D | E |

STAY ON THE SUBJECT!

Objective: Present ideas that are relevant to the subject and in a logical sequence.

Activities Covered

- Writing words under headings
- Using numbers to show order
- Discussing ideas
- Demonstrating how to do something to the class

Background Information

In this lesson, students must stay focused on the subject at hand only, and must not be diverted!

Students will also have some practice in ordering their ideas.

Before the Lesson

The teacher can use an example of how we stay on the subject by introducing a topic—for example, a visit to the beach—and students can give words that match the topic. The teacher could write words on the board, and some ordering could be done after all the words have been written down; for example, 1. car trip 2. sand 3. swim 4. sandcastle 5. shells 6. picnic.

Students must be given time to prepare for their demonstration.

The Lesson (Pages 35 and 36)

Have a class discussion as mentioned above.

Under the given headings, students write down words that have something to do with the topics.

Students number their words. (This ordering of thoughts can be general, as long as their ordering makes sense.)

Students write numbers next to sentences about a school project to place them in correct sequence.

Students discuss all their answers with the class.

Once students have been given time to prepare and practice, they will demonstrate something to the class; for example, how to plant a seed, how to brush your teeth correctly, how to peel an apple. Students should preferably bring items to school to best explain their demonstration.

Students assess their demonstration by answering the given questions.

Answers

1. Answers will vary, but possible lists of words for each task include:
    Packing for a Trip: suitcase, clothing, toiletries, passports, money, towels, book, medication, locks, tickets, etc.
    Making a Cheese Sandwich: bread, butter, cheese, butter knife, plate, bread knife, etc.
    Getting Ready for School: breakfast, teeth, uniform, schoolbag, shoes, socks, hairbrush, lunchbox, homework, face, etc.
2. Teacher check
3. Answers may vary, but a good answer is 5, 6, 7, 1, 2, 4, 3.
4.–6. Teacher check

Additional Activities

Students or the teacher can demonstrate a particular type of dance to the rest of the class, and the class must follow.

The students can look at maps of their local area and map out the best routes to get to particular places.

Students can write relevant lists of words for topics in geography and history and display these in the classroom.

Students can pretend to take important visitors around the school, concentrating on the sequence.

Students can look at first aid procedures and experiment with practicing them.

Students can read the following poem about a family member, then write their own shorter poem about one of their family members.

My Great Grandma

My great grandma,
She likes to bake
Sweet apple pie
And chocolate cake.

My great grandma
Has always time
To tell a tale,
Recite a rhyme.

My great grandma,
She laughs a lot
And cheers up folks
Who time forgot.

My great grandma,
She's like a mate.
I love her so.
My grandma's great!

Stay On the Subject!

Try to focus on the topics and don't get sidetracked!

1 Under these headings, write words that have something to do with the task.

Packing for a Trip	Making a Cheese Sandwich	Getting Ready for School

2 Write numbers next to your words to show what order they could be done in.

3 Write numbers next to these sentences to show what order they should be done in.

How to Complete a School Project

☐ Write your notes out neatly.

☐ Write your project neatly.

☐ Add pictures and color to your project.

☐ Do a rough draft of your plan for your project.

☐ Look in the library for suitable books.

☐ Make a list of the books you used.

☐ Do your research and make rough notes.

4 Discuss all your answers with the class.

Stay On the Subject!

(5) You are going to give a demonstration to your class. Your demonstration can be about anything you want. Here are some ideas.

- How to juggle
- How to make a banana milkshake
- How to tie your shoelaces
- How to brush your teeth
- How to thread a needle
- How to sharpen a pencil

(a) I am going to demonstrate how to _____

_____

(b) What items could you bring to school to help with your demonstration?

_____

_____

(c) Write notes to show the order of your demonstration.

1	2
3	4
5	6

(6) Once you have given your demonstration, answer these questions.

(a) How well did your demonstration go?

_____

_____

(b) How could you have improved it?

_____

_____

_____

_____

MAKE IT SHORT AND SWEET!

Objective: Summarize and prioritize ideas.

Activities Covered

- Discussing summarizing
- Summarizing sentences
- Writing description, summarizing and reading it

Background Information

The word "summarize" must first be explained to students. The teacher should tell students that to summarize means to make the text shorter by using only the most important facts. The teacher could discuss with the class the fact that we summarize information on a daily basis anyway, because we cannot take in all the information that is part of our everyday lives.

Before the Lesson

The teacher can have examples of how we summarize in daily life. For example, if a parent asked what his or her child did at school, the student wouldn't explain every minute, but would say he/she did art, played football and did experiments in science. Students can come up with other times when we might summarize; for example, taking messages, writing down homework, describing experiences.

The teacher can also have examples on how to summarize written text. For example, "The naughty, eleven-year-old boy forgot to do his homework for the third time in a row. The teacher, who was extremely angry, decided to call his parents to try to sort the matter out." could be summarized as "The naughty student had forgotten his homework three times and the teacher called his parents."

The Lesson (Pages 38 and 39)

Have a class discussion as mentioned above.

Students summarize the sentences given on the sheet. (The teacher can explain to the class that the words can be changed if necessary, it is the meaning that must stay the same).

As a class, students discuss their answers to Questions 1 and 2.

Students write a description of their family.

Students summarize their description.

Students read their summary to the class.

Students summarize their day so far by writing two sentences.

Answers

1. Answers will vary, but could include:
    - (a) The house belonged to a witch, and it was said she cast spells there.
    - (b) The cat stalked the mouse, which was unaware of the danger.
    - (c) My mother insisted I wear the horrible sweater.
    - (d) I didn't want to join the Halloween celebrations, as I was afraid and didn't want candy.
2. Answers will vary, but could include:
    10 pages of reading book, spelling test on Friday, p. 35 of math book, x6 test on Monday, Roman roads worksheet
3.–7. Teacher check

Additional Activities

In pairs, students look at a chore list that their mother may have written. The students must decide what order the chores should be done in.

Summarize a given poem. Any poem can be used provided that the main ideas can be summarized.

Make it Short and Sweet!

Summarizing means to make something shorter, using only the most important information.

1 Summarize these passages.

(a) The white house belonged to what people called an old and wicked witch. She was said to cast spells there and turn teachers into frogs!

_____

_____

(b) The fluffy, fat cat slowly and carefully stalked the little, gray field mouse. The mouse did not know it was being followed so closely.

_____

_____

(c) My mother insisted I wear the horrible, blue sweater. It had been knitted by an ancient aunt of mine, who wasn't up to date with the latest fashions.

_____

_____

Use only the main facts!

(d) I didn't want to join the Halloween celebrations. I was terrified of all the kids in costumes, who I couldn't recognize. In any case, I didn't like candy, so what was the point?

_____

_____

2 Your teacher has a very long list of homework for you! Summarize the homework on the notepad.

You need to read 10 pages of your reading book, learn your spelling for a test on Friday, complete the sums on page 35 of your math book, learn your 6 times table for a test on Monday, and finish your history worksheet about Roman roads, if you have not already finished it!

My Homework

_____

_____

_____

_____

_____

_____

3 Discuss your answers with your class.

Make it Short and Sweet!

4 Write a detailed description of your family.

_____

_____

_____

_____

_____

_____

_____

_____

5 Now summarize it!

_____

_____

_____

_____

_____

6 Read your summary to the class!

7 Summarize your day so far in two sentences.

_____

_____

_____

WISE WORDS

Objective: Discuss the meaning of proverbs with the teacher.

Activities Covered

- **Group Work** – writing meanings of proverbs
- **Class Work** – discussing meanings of proverbs
- Matching beginnings and endings of proverbs
- Using a proverb in a sentence

Background Information

This lesson contains proverbs, but other lessons should be done whereby the students and teacher discuss local expressions and words and their possible origins. Students need to have practice in using expressions and proverbs orally, so the teacher should encourage students to use them in their conversations for that week. The teacher should also encourage the use of these in students' writing activities.

Before the Lesson

The teacher should have a collection of proverbs/sayings/expressions not included in the lesson. The teacher can look at websites to get some examples. See the list in the *Additional Activities* section.

The class will be divided into groups.

The Lesson (Pages 41 and 42)

The teacher discusses with students the proverbs and sayings he/she has brought in. Teachers can explain to students what a proverb is (a wise saying) and give examples of everyday expressions; for example, about time, all ears, calm down, crocodile tears, eat like a bird, eyes in the back of her head.

Group Work – Students listen to the teacher use each proverb in context (see *Answers* for examples); then the group must discuss and write down what they think the proverb means.

Each group's answers are discussed as a class.

Students match beginnings and endings of proverbs.

These must then be discussed with the class, and students can suggest ideas for what they mean and how they may have originated.

Students write one proverb and its meaning.

Students draw an illustration of the proverb.

Answers

1. The teacher could use the following sentences to illustrate each proverb in context:
   (a) I am going to be the first person at the sale tomorrow, as the early bird catches the worm.
   (b) I am starting my project early and am going to work on it every day, as a stitch in time saves nine.
   (c) You might not get that CD player for your birthday, so don't count your chickens before they hatch.
   (d) I have explained to my brother how to learn his nine times tables, but he will not listen—you can lead a horse to water but you cannot make it drink.

   (e) The teacher warned you that you would be punished if you forgot your homework again; you made your bed, so you must lie in it.
   (f) The robber jumped out of the frying pan and into the fire when he ran from the police into a fierce guard dog.
   (g) That group of girls is always getting into trouble, as birds of a feather flock together.
   (h) It would be better if just one person painted the art project, as too many cooks spoil the broth.
2. Teacher check
3. (a) He who makes no mistakes, makes nothing.
   (b) A bad workman always blames his tools.
   (c) A fool and his money are soon parted.
   (d) All that glitters is not gold.
   (e) All work and no play makes Jack a dull boy.
   (f) A rolling stone gathers no moss.
   (g) There is no fireside like your own fireside.
   (h) A friend in need is a friend indeed.
   (i) He who runs away lives to fight another day.
   (j) Praise the young and they will blossom.
4.–6. Teacher check

Additional Activities

The teacher can discuss with students the origins of certain words and how we have borrowed words from other languages; for example, terra firma, chateau. These can be displayed in the classroom, perhaps on a map of the world to show where the words originate.

This same type of lesson can be done with common phrases, sayings and expressions.

Students can each be given one proverb/expression and they must draw a picture to show the meaning. These can be displayed in the classroom.

Students can have conversations in pairs, using as many expressions/proverbs as they can.

Students can read poetry that makes use of common expressions. For example:

Misunderstood

"Oh, no!" said Tom, "My goose is fried!"
"Oh, don't say that!" the teacher cried.

"Don't you know fried food is bad?
Haven't you heard of cholesterol, lad?

"The food pyramid does clearly show
We must keep fat intake low!

"Otherwise, you'll get obese,
And all because of your fried geese!

"Now, boy, you must use the grill
So your arteries don't feel ill!

"You can bake and steam and boil,
And always use pure olive oil!

"I hope you've taken all this in.
Fatty foods go in the bin!"

"No, Miss, I really get you not,
It's just my homework I forgot."

Wise Words

Using expressions and proverbs can make our conversation more interesting.

She's jumping from the frying pan into the fire!

1 Listen to your teacher. As a group, discuss and write down what you think these proverbs mean.

(a) The early bird catches the worm.

_____

_____

_____

(b) A stitch in time saves nine.

_____

_____

_____

(c) Don't count your chickens before they hatch.

_____

_____

_____

(d) You can lead a horse to water but you can't make it drink.

_____

_____

_____

(e) As you make your bed, so must you lie in it.

_____

_____

(f) Out of the frying pan and into the fire.

_____

_____

(g) Birds of a feather flock together.

_____

_____

(h) Too many cooks spoil the broth.

_____

_____

2 Discuss the meaning of each proverb as a class.

Wise Words

There is a time to speak and a time to be silent!

③ Match up the beginnings and endings of these proverbs.

(a) He who makes no mistakes •   • makes Jack a dull boy.

(b) A bad workman •   • like your own fireside.

(c) A fool and his money •   • always blames his tools.

(d) All that glitters •   • lives to fight another day.

(e) All work and no play •   • are soon parted.

(f) A rolling stone •   • is not gold.

(g) There is no fireside •   • makes nothing.

(h) A friend in need •   • gathers no moss.

(i) He who runs away •   • and they will blossom.

(j) Praise the young •   • is a friend indeed.

④ Discuss all of the above with the class.

⑤ (a) Choose a proverb and write it down.

_____

(b) Write the proverb's meaning.

_____

_____

⑥ Draw an illustration of the proverb.

NEW WORDS

Objective: Become aware of new words and new connotations of words through his/her reading and writing experience.

Activities Covered

- **Group Work –** reading sentences, guessing meaning of words
- Discussing answers with the class
- Guessing word meanings and checking using a dictionary
- Deciding which words are used in the correct context
- Replacing words with correct meanings
- Using new words in oral sentences

Background Information

In this lesson, students will be hearing new and unfamiliar words and they must be used in context. Students must get clues from reading the sentence as to what each new word means. All new words can be added to their personal wordbook or spelling journal. This type of lesson can be done over and over again, using different lists of new and more challenging words. The words are not only to be used in this lesson—remind students when they are speaking or have a writing activity to try to incorporate some of the new words. The words can be displayed in the classroom to remind students—one section of the wall can be the "word wall." The teacher should use the new words too!

Before the Lesson

The teacher can have lists of other words to be discussed.

The class will be divided into groups.

The Lesson (Pages 44 and 45)

Group Work – Students try to guess the meanings of the underlined words by getting clues from the sentence.

Groups discuss their answers with the rest of the class. (Students can at this point use the new words in their own oral sentences.)

Group Work – Students guess meanings of words. Then they can look them up in the dictionary to check whether they were correct.

Groups discuss their answers with the rest of the class.

Students decide which words have been used in the correct context and change incorrect words by using a word that has been learned in the lesson.

After all new words have been discussed, students can use the new words in oral sentences.

Answers

1.–2. Answers will vary, but could include:
- (a) someone who eats too much/is greedy
- (b) find   (c) hang around
- (d) crack/split (e) nervous/anxious
- (f) smell   (g) longed   (h) crushed
- (i) choose   (j) lift/put up (k) bird of prey
- (l) field

3.–5. Teacher check

6. (a) Leave the ice cream to thaw out.
- (b) The brash pupil got into trouble.
- (c) Did you locate your homework?
- (d) Before he robbed the bank, the thief had to loiter outside.
- (e) Eating vegetables is vital for your health.
- (f) The students yearned for their holiday.
- (g) Did you opt for blue or black shoes?
- (h) The savage dog barked and snarled.
- (i) The eagle made a nest high on the cliff.
- (j) The gate to the paddock had been broken.

7. Teacher check

Additional Activities

Students can read a passage given by the teacher and replace each underlined word with one from a list of more challenging words.

The teacher can introduce students to more challenging words. Students must guess the meanings when the teacher uses them in a sentence.

The teacher can tell the students a few interesting words; for example, hornswoggle (to cheat, hoax) or roo (to pluck the wool from the fleece of a sheep). Strange words should be introduced for fun and not for learning!

Students should be shown how to access the dictionary when they are working on the computer.

New Words

You will learn some new words in this lesson.

Use them in your conversation and writing.

Using these words will make you sound very intelligent!

(1) Work with your group to read the sentences. Write down what you think the underlined word means.

(a) My brother is a **glutton**. He had four hamburgers for lunch!

_____

(b) I cannot **locate** my new shoes. I don't know where I left them!

_____

(c) Students are not allowed to **loiter** at the school gate.

_____

(d) The sheep fell down the **fissure** in the rock.

_____

(e) I felt **jittery** before giving my speech.

_____

(f) The **scent** of the baking bread is making me hungry.

_____

(g) The sailor **yearned** for the sea.

_____

(h) A macaroon is made of **ground** almonds and sugar.

_____

(i) I will **opt** to go to the movie theater instead of the store.

_____

(j) If you **raise** your hand I will listen to you.

_____

(k) The **eagle** circled before pouncing on the mouse.

_____

(l) The horse galloped around the **paddock**.

_____

(2) Discuss the meanings with your class.

(3) How many did your group get right out of 12? ☐

(4) Still in your groups, use a dictionary to find out what these words mean.

frail, savage, plead, exit, cling, vital, thaw, brash, drab, meek

(5) Discuss the meanings with your class.

Did you know?

Naughty students in the 1700s who enjoyed breaking windows were called "nickers"!

New Words

6 Read the sentences. They do not make sense. Replace the incorrect words, choosing new words you have learned, from the word bank below.

	Sentence	Incorrect Word	Correct New Word
(a)	Leave the ice cream to scent out.	scent	thaw
(b)	The meek pupil got into trouble.		
(c)	Did you plead your homework?		
(d)	Before he robbed the bank, the thief had to fissure outside.		
(e)	Eating vegetables is drab for your health.		
(f)	The students jittery for their holiday.		
(g)	Did you raise for blue or black shoes?		
(h)	The cling dog barked and snarled.		
(i)	The ground made a nest high on the cliff.		
(j)	The gate to the glutton had been broken.		

WORD BANK

brash	ground	meek	savage
cling	jittery	opt	scent
drab	eagle	paddock	thaw
fissure	locate	plead	vital
glutton	loiter	raise	yearned

7 Use all the new words in oral sentences!

OPPOSITE OR NOT?

Objective: Play synonym and antonym games.

Activities Covered

- **Group Work –** finding synonyms
- Discussing answers with class
- Adding up scores
- Writing antonyms
- Class voting for best sentences

Background Information

Before the lesson, the words "synonym" and "antonym" must first be explained to the class. The teacher can give examples and get students to come up with some of their own. It should be pointed out that words often have more than one meaning; for example, bad – "The boy is bad" – meaning naughty, or "The fruit is bad" – meaning rotten.

Before the Lesson

The teacher can have examples of antonyms and synonyms.

Students will be divided into groups.

The Lesson (Pages 47 and 48)

Group work – Students try to come up with as many synonyms as they can for the given words. The teacher can explain to the students that the more synonyms they list, the more points they are likely to get.

Once the time is up (the teacher can decide when), students discuss their synonyms with the rest of the class. If only a particular group has that synonym, they get 10 points for that synonym. If other groups have it too, they get 5 points for that synonym. The teacher will need to make sure that the synonyms are correct.

Groups add up their points and a winner is announced.

Students write antonyms for given words in sentences.

These sentences are read to the class and the class votes for the top six sentences.

Students read the passage, write an antonym for each underlined word, and then reread the passage using the antonyms.

Answers

1. Answers will vary, but could include:
    (a) cross, annoyed, irritated, vexed, fuming, outraged, furious
    (b) soggy, damp, dripping, soaked, drenched, sopping, moist
    (c) bold, mischievous, bad, disobedient, wicked, impish, wayward
    (d) ill, unwell, poorly, off-color, ailing, bad
    (e) naughty, rotten, horrible, awful, terrible, unpleasant, dreadful
    (f) little, petite, undersized, miniature, minute, tiny
    (g) adore, worship, care for, feel affection for
    (h) see, watch, observe, seem, appear
    (i) frightening, creepy, chilling, terrifying
    (j) insane, cross, silly, foolish, crazy
    (k) intelligent, bright, smart, quick, witty, brainy, sharp
    (l) unclean, grubby, filthy, grimy, mucky, soiled, polluted
    (m) earnest, grave, serious, sober, thoughtful, glum, formal, dignified
    (n) bashful, coy, hesitant, cautious, nervous, reticent, self-conscious, timid, wary
2. Teacher check
3. Answers will vary, but could include:
    (a) The stiff jelly tasted disgusting.
    (b) The beautiful frog turned into a grotesque prince.
    (c) The enormous lady hit the kind man.
    (d) Tom cried loudly when he passed the test.
    (e) The teacher was happy when the student was good.
    (f) The dog was spotless after walking through the forest.
4. Teacher check.
5. Answers will vary, but could include:
    short, happy, young, bald, gentle, beautiful, tiny, sunny, short, scruffy, loudly, dirty, attractive, messed-up, bottom, top, disgusting, sad

Additional Activities

Students can have a "synonym and antonym race" in groups, where each group gets given a list to find. The class can discuss them afterwards.

Students can change the meanings of poems/short stories by writing antonyms for particular words.

Opposite or Not?

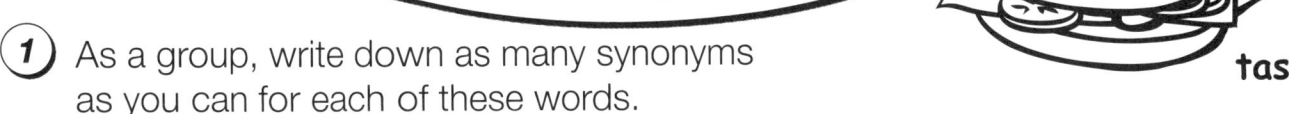

Synonyms are words with a similar meaning.
Antonyms are words that have an opposite meaning.

yummy   delicious

tasty

1 As a group, write down as many synonyms as you can for each of these words.

(a) angry _____

(b) wet _____

(c) naughty _____

(d) sick _____

(e) bad _____

(f) small _____

(g) love _____

(h) look _____

(i) scary _____

(j) mad _____

(k) clever _____

(l) dirty _____

(m) solemn _____

(n) shy _____

2 (a) Discuss your synonyms with the class. If only your group had that particular synonym, your group gets 10 points. If other groups had it too, your group gets 5 points for that synonym. See which group had the most points!

(b) How many points did your group get?

(c) What was the highest score?

School is great! How many synonyms can you think of for "great"?

Opposite or Not?

3 As a group, write antonyms for each of the underlined words.

(a) The <u>wobbly</u> jelly tasted <u>delicious</u>.

The _____ jelly

tasted _____.

(c) The <u>tiny</u> lady hit the <u>unkind</u> man.

The _____ lady hit

the _____ man.

(e) The teacher was <u>angry</u> when the student was <u>naughty</u>.

The teacher was

_____ when the

student was _____.

4 (a) Read your sentences to your class.

(b) Have a class vote for the six best sentences.

5 Read the passage. Write an antonym for every underlined word. Read the passage again, using the antonyms.

Antonyms

1. _____   10. _____

2. _____   11. _____

3. _____   12. _____

4. _____   13. _____

5. _____   14. _____

6. _____   15. _____

7. _____   16. _____

8. _____   17. _____

9. _____   18. _____

(b) The <u>ugly</u> frog turned into a <u>handsome</u> prince.

The _____ frog

turned into a _____

prince.

(d) Tom cried <u>softly</u> when he <u>failed</u> the test.

Tom cried _____

when he _____ the

test.

(f) The dog was <u>dirty</u> after <u>running</u> through the forest.

The dog was _____

after _____ through

the forest.

Once upon a time, a <u>long</u>[1] time ago, there lived a <u>miserable</u>[2], <u>old</u>[3] king and his <u>hairy</u>[4], <u>vicious</u>[5] dog. They lived in a <u>hideous</u>[6], <u>huge</u>[7] castle. One <u>rainy</u>[8] day, two <u>tall</u>[9], <u>immaculate</u>[10] men knocked <u>gently</u>[11] on the door. They had come to <u>clean</u>[12] the castle, as there was a <u>disgusting</u>[13] smell. They <u>cleaned</u>[14] the castle from <u>top</u>[15] to <u>bottom</u>[16]. Soon the castle smelled <u>lovely</u>[17] and the king became very <u>happy</u>[18].

NAMING OR DOING?

Objective: Become familiar with the functions of words without necessarily using technical grammatical terms.

Activities Covered

- Writing sentences
- Identifying verbs and nouns
- Reading and listening to sentences
- Completing sentences as a group
- Reading sentences to the class
- Voting for favorite sentences

Background Information

This lesson concentrates on nouns and verbs only, so as not to bombard students with all the parts of speech. Each should be discussed separately and much practice given. Depending on the class, it is up to the teacher whether he/she uses the terms "noun" and "verb" or "naming word" and "doing/action word."

Before the Lesson

The teacher must have examples of nouns and verbs that can be discussed with the class. These should also be shown in sentences, and examples should be left on the board so students can refer to them when they answer questions on their sheet.

The class will be divided into pairs and then groups.

The Lesson (Pages 50 and 51)

The teacher explains the difference between verbs and nouns and asks students for examples of each. These can be written on the board under headings.

The teacher gives the students a few sentences, and students must identify the nouns and verbs in each sentence.

Students write sentences on their sheet using the given nouns and verbs.

Students circle the nouns and verbs in their sentences, using two different color crayons.

Students read their sentences to their partners. Partners need to identify the nouns and verbs.

Groups complete the sentences, trying to make their sentences funny.

Groups read their sentences to the class.

The class votes for the funniest sentence and all groups write it on their sheet.

Students discuss the nouns and verbs in each group's sentences.

Answers

1. Answers will vary. Here are some examples:
   (a) The boy gobbled his dinner in three seconds.
   (b) The elephant squashed all the hot dogs for our picnic.
   (c) The ghost screamed when he saw my sister come into the room.
   (d) Santa tripped over Rudolph's reins and all the presents went flying through the air.
   (e) The teacher snoozed while the quiet class got on with their work.
   (f) The fierce dog growled when he heard the intruder.
   (g) The athlete was delighted when the crowd cheered.
   (h) The big, hungry dinosaur chased the smaller dinosaur.
2.–5. Teacher check

Additional Activities

The same type of lesson can be done with other parts of speech; for example, adjectives, adverbs, pronouns, prepositions, different types of nouns.

Students can write lists of nouns and verbs for different topics in different subjects; for example, geography or history.

Naming or Doing?

1 Write sentences using the given words.

> Naming words are called nouns.
> A noun names an object, place, or person; for example, school, Peter, pencil, France.
>
> Doing words are called verbs. A verb describes an action; for example, run, write, eat, dance.

(a) boy, gobbled

_____

_____

_____

(b) elephant, squashed

_____

_____

(c) ghost, screamed

_____

_____

(d) Santa, tripped

_____

_____

(e) teacher, snoozed

_____

_____

(f) dog, growled

_____

_____

(g) athlete, cheered

_____

_____

(h) dinosaur, chased

_____

_____

2 In each sentence:

(a) Circle the naming words **(nouns)**, using a red pencil.

(b) Circle the doing words **(verbs)**, using a blue pencil.

3 Read each sentence to your partner. Can he or she tell you which words are the nouns and verbs?

Naming or Doing?

4 Work with your group. Write funny sentences using the given words.

(a) The grumpy teacher

_____

_____

_____

(b) The fierce dragon _____

_____

_____

_____

(c) The enormous elephant

_____

_____

_____

(d) My little brother _____

_____

_____

_____

(e) My mad cat _____

_____

_____

_____

(f) The crazy scientist _____

_____

_____

_____

(g) The smiling baby _____

_____

_____

_____

(h) The angry ant _____

_____

_____

_____

5 (a) Read your sentences to your class.

(b) Hold a class vote to decide the funniest sentence.

(c) Write the funniest sentence here.

_____

_____

(d) Circle the nouns in red pencil and the verbs in blue pencil.

MIND YOUR MANNERS!

Objective: Practice the common social functions in the everyday context of class and school and through improvisational drama.

Activities Covered

- Responding to different situations in writing and through role-play
- Deciding which comments are suitable (polite and impolite)
- Discussing answers with the class
- Suggesting polite and impolite ways of responding to situations
- **Pair Work –** role-playing situations

Background Information

This lesson makes students aware of certain social functions, such as introducing someone, thanking a person for a gift, and saying things in a polite and inoffensive way. The best way for students to learn the correct way is through role-play and watching others. Discussion in this lesson is important. This type of lesson can be done again and again, focusing each time on a different social function.

Before the Lesson

The teacher can have similar examples ready to present to the students for discussion.

The class will be divided into pairs.

The Lesson (Pages 53 and 54)

Students respond to situations on their sheet by writing a polite reply.

Students role-play responding to situations in a polite manner.

Students decide which statements are impolite.

Students discuss ways of making impolite statements polite.

Pair Work – Students role-play a choice of situations in both a polite and impolite manner and perform them for the class.

Answers

1. Answers will vary. Here are some examples:
   (a) "I really like your project—you have worked so hard on it."
   (b) "What is the matter? Is there anything I can help you with?"
   (c) "Thank you very much for the lovely gift. I have wanted this book for ages!"
   (d) "Mrs. Brown, may I introduce my parents, Mr. and Mrs. Cook?"
   (e) "Thank you for taking me to the movies. I really enjoyed the film."
   (f) "Mmm! Thanks, Dad, this is yummy!"
2. Teacher check
3.–4. (a) polite
   (b) impolite; "Your poster is colorful, but there are a few words that I can't clearly read."
   (c) impolite; "Thank you for the pen."
   (d) impolite; "Your shoes look good on you, but I prefer black ones."
   (e) impolite; "I'm sorry I can't come to your house today, but I've already made plans. Could we do it another day?"
   (f) impolite; "Thanks for cooking, Mom, but this is not one of my favorite dishes."
   (g) polite
5. Teacher check

Additional Activities

This same lesson can be done with other social functions; for example, expressing disapproval, taking part in simple commercial transactions (playing store), asking questions to get views and feelings, showing support, and giving directions.

Students can discuss how they can be polite in the classroom and playground.

Mind Your Manners!

You should always be polite.
Say "please" and "thank you" often!

1 Work with your partner to discuss and write what you should say in these situations.

(a) You think your friend's project is very good. " _____

_____ "

(b) Your sister looks sad. " _____

_____ "

(c) Your aunt gives you a book that you have always wanted.

" _____

_____ "

(d) Your parents meet your teacher for the first time.

" _____

_____ "

(e) Your friend's parents take you to the movies.

" _____

_____ "

(f) Your Dad buys you an ice cream for helping in the garden.

" _____

_____ "

2 (a) Choose one of these situations to perform for your class.

(b) Decide who will be which character.

• I will be _____

• My partner will be _____

(c) Work out what each of you will say and do. Practice!

(d) Perform your role-play. Color the stars to assess your performance.

1 2 3 4 5

Did you know?
If you greet someone in India, you should place your palms together as though praying and bend or nod. This is called namaste.

Mind Your Manners!

3 Work with your partner to read and discuss what these people have said. Write an "X" in the box if they have said the wrong thing.

(a) "Thanks for the new shirt, Mom. I really like it."
☐

(b) "Your poster is colorful, but it's so messy I can hardly read it."
☐

(c) "I don't need this pen you gave me but thanks anyway."
☐

There is no excuse for bad manners!

(d) "I don't think your shoes are cool at all!"
☐

(e) "No, I don't think I'll come to your house today as I'd prefer to go to Harry's."
☐

(f) "Please, Mom, don't make this spinach dish again; it's too dreadful!"
☐

(g) "I'd love to come to your party, but I have to go to a wedding instead."
☐

4 As a class, discuss your answers to Question 3. Suggest how some of the impolite ones could be made polite.

5 (a) With your partner, choose one of these situations.

You are working on your science project and need the glue. However, someone else on your table has the glue.

You go to your friend's house for dinner, but the meal includes peas. You really don't like peas!

Your friend asks you to go ice skating on Saturday, but you have already arranged to go to the movies with another friend.

(b) Check the situation you have chosen.

(c) Write how you could respond in a polite manner. _____

_____

(d) Write how you could respond in an impolite manner. _____

_____

(e) Work with your partner to role-play how you could respond in a polite and an impolite manner.

(f) Perform your role-plays for your class.

EXPRESS IT!

Objective: Make lists of local expressions and words.

Activities Covered

- Researching a local expression/word
- Discussing word with the class
- Filling in place names
- Discussing possible origins of names
- Matching expressions to their meanings
- Writing meanings of expressions
- Using expressions in conversation

Background Information

It is important that lists of local and general expressions are displayed in the classroom to remind students of what has been discussed. The lists should be referred to every now and then, and students should be encouraged to use the expressions in their conversations and writing.

Before the Lesson

The students must bring to class a local or general expression.

The teacher should also prepare a list of common expressions.

The class will be divided into pairs.

The teacher can do some research on the origins of place and family names for Question 3.

The Lesson (Pages 56 and 57)

Students tell the class their expression and what they think it means.

Students fill in names as requested.

As a class, students discuss the possible origins of these names.

Students write down what they think the expressions on the list mean.

Pair Work – Students use as many expressions as they can in a conversation.

Answers

1.–5.   Teacher check.
6.   (a) Wish me luck!
     (b) I'm listening.
     (c) I have no clothes on!
7.   (a) You saved me!
     (b) I love sausages.
     (c) Sleep well!
     (d) He looked at me in a mean/nasty way.
     (e) You eat a lot.
     (f) You eat so little.
     (g) My teacher always seems to know what is going on.
     (h) Don't shout at me!
     (i) You will find yourself in trouble.
     (j) At last!

Additional Activities

Students can each receive one expression and they can make a drawing that depicts it. The expression should be written with the drawing. These can be displayed in the classroom.

Students can write sentences using the expressions.

Express It!

Expressions are like sayings. For example: "The teacher went mad!" usually means that the teacher was very angry, not that the teacher went insane. (Hopefully!)

DIG IN!

1 For homework you had to find a common expression.

What expression did you find? _____

_____

2 What does it mean? _____

_____

3 Name the following:

(a) The area you live in:

_____

_____

(b) Your school:

_____

_____

(c) A street in your town:

_____

_____

(d) A building:

_____

_____

4 Discuss with the class where these names may have originated.

(e) Your family name:

_____

_____

5 Research one of the names you used in Question 3.

(a) I have chosen _____

(b) Write about how this name may have originated.

_____

_____

Express It!

6 Match these expressions to their meanings.

(a) Keep your fingers crossed!   •   •   I have no clothes on!

(b) I'm all ears!   •   •   Wish me luck!

(c) I am in my birthday suit!   •   •   I'm listening!

7 Work with your partner to discuss and write down what you think these expressions mean.

(a) You saved my bacon! _____

_____

(b) I'm crazy about sausages! _____

_____

(c) Good night! Don't let the bed bugs bite! _____

_____

(d) He gave me a dirty look. _____

_____

(e) You eat like a horse. _____

_____

(f) You eat like a bird. _____

_____

(g) My teacher has eyes in the back of her head. _____

_____

(h) Don't bite my head off! _____

_____

(i) You will land in deep water. _____

_____

(j) It's about time! _____

_____

8 Have a conversation with your partner and try to use as many expressions as you can.

RHYME TIME

Objective: Use improvisational drama to re-create well-known characters.

Activities Covered

- Acting out a nursery rhyme in a group of five or six
- Acting out a nursery rhyme in a group of two or three
- Assessing performances

Background Information

Nursery rhymes have been used in this lesson, but any characters with whom the students are familiar are suitable, such as characters in well-known stories or characters in the class reader.

Before the Lesson

The teacher can have an example of a nursery rhyme and how it will be acted out.

The class will be divided into groups of five or six students.

Later in the lesson, each group will be split into two groups of two or three students.

A selection of nursery rhymes containing two or three parts (characters) will need to be available.

The Lesson (Pages 54 and 55)

The teacher can use an example of a nursery rhyme and how it could be acted out. (See suggestion in *Answers*.)

The teacher gives each group a nursery rhyme from the sheet.

Students answer questions on the sheet.

Groups practice acting out their rhyme, perform it to their class and assess their performance.

Students choose and write out another rhyme to act out.

Students practice acting out their second rhyme, perform it for their class and assess their performance.

Answers

1.–3.   Teacher check

Possible example for the teacher:

Three blind mice (three students acting as blind mice, perhaps bumping into things, etc.)

Three blind mice.
See how they run, see how they run. *(students running around)*
They all ran after the farmer's wife, *(one student is the angry farmer's wife)*
Who cut off their tails with a carving knife, *(waving her arms around, trying to catch them)*
Did you ever see such a thing in your life, *(perhaps a few spectators, shaking their heads, spurring them on)*
As three blind mice! *(three tailless mice)*

Students can add their own ideas to the rhymes; their acting does not have to follow the rhyme strictly.

Additional Activities

Students can use improvisational drama to recreate a favorite TV program, parts of films, cartoons, etc.

Rhyme Time

1 In your group, choose one of these nursery rhymes.

Can you remember some nursery rhymes?

Humpty Dumpty

Humpty Dumpty sat on a wall,

Humpty Dumpty had a great fall;

All the King's horses,

And all the King's men,

Couldn't put Humpty together again.

Hey, Diddle, Diddle

Hey, diddle, diddle

The cat and the fiddle,

The cow jumped over the moon.

The little dog laughed

To see such sport,

And the dish ran away with

the spoon.

Old King Cole

Old King Cole was a merry old soul,

And a merry old soul was he;

He called for his pipe,

And he called for his bowl,

And he called for his fiddlers three.

Every fiddler he had a fiddle,

And a very fine fiddle had he;

Oh, there's none so rare

As can compare

With King Cole and his fiddlers three.

Georgie Porgie

Georgie Porgie,

Pudding and pie,

Kissed the girls

And made them cry.

When the boys

Came out to play,

Georgie Porgie

Ran away.

Why do you think they are called "nursery" rhymes?

Rhyme Time

2 Your group is going to act out a nursery rhyme! Say the rhyme as you act it out. Each member in the group must have a part to play!

(a) Which rhyme has your group chosen to act out? _____

(b) Write the names of the students in your group and their roles.

Name	Role

(c) Perform your nursery rhyme for your class.

(d) Color how well your group acted (5 is the best!).

3 Split your group into two separate groups, each containing two or three students. Each group is going to choose and act out a different nursery rhyme. Each member in the group must have a part to play!

(a) Which rhyme has your group chosen to act out? _____

(b) Write the nursery rhyme here.

(c) Write the names of the students in your group and their roles.

Name	Role

(d) Perform your nursery rhyme for your class.

(e) Color how well your group acted.

| 1 | 2 | 3 | 4 | 5 |

LISTEN TO A STORY!

Objective: Hear, discuss and react to local storytellers.

Activities Covered

- Listening to a storyteller
- Discussing a story
- Answering questions
- Drawing a picture
- Explaining drawing to the class

Background Information

It might prove to be a problem to get a local storyteller to come to the school. If the teacher doesn't know of any, he/she should contact the local arts council. If there are no storytellers available, the teacher should ask someone from the local community who would be suitable. The teacher should explain to the students beforehand who the storyteller is. Teachers could discuss storytelling before the lesson, and the class can decide if storytellers would still be in demand in today's times and why/why not.

Before the Lesson

The teacher needs to locate a storyteller!

The Lesson (Pages 62 and 63)

The teacher could discuss the art and history of storytelling with the students before this lesson.

The teacher must explain to the class who the storyteller is.

Students listen to the story.

Students ask the storyteller questions about the story.

Students discuss the story.

Students answer questions on their sheet about the story.

Students discuss some of their answers with their class.

Students draw a picture that depicts the story.

Students show and describe their picture to the class.

Answers

Teacher check

Additional Activities

The teacher can read different short stories and the class can discuss them.

The teacher can read different poems (for example: funny, disgusting, charming, sad) to the class and students can give their reactions.

The class could decide what qualities a storyteller should have.

Students can retell the story they heard to a family member.

The website: *www.42explore.com* contains information for teachers.

Listen to a Story!

> Listen to the story the storyteller tells and then answer these questions.

1 Who was the storyteller? _____

2 What was the story called? _____

3 What was the story about? _____

_____

_____

_____

4 Where was the story set? _____

5 When was the story set? _____

6 Who were the main characters? Describe them briefly. _____

_____

_____

> Did you know? LISTEN has the same letters in it as SILENT.

7 (a) Did it have a good ending?   yes   no

(b) Why?/Why not? _____

_____

_____

8 What part did you enjoy most and why? _____

_____

_____

_____

9 Discuss your answers to Question 8 with your class. Have a vote on your favorite part of the story. Which part did most students enjoy the most?

_____

_____

Listen to a Story!

(10) Draw a picture that depicts part of the story.

(11) Show your picture to the class and explain it.

Did you know?

In ancient times, it was the custom in each Irish village to start the Celtic New Year on November the 1st with storytelling every night, until May brought the summer back.

LOOK IT UP!

Objective: Use simple dictionaries effectively.

Activities Covered

- Matching pictures and words
- Looking in dictionaries
- Writing sentences containing given words in the correct context
- Drawing pictures to show meaning
- Discussing answers (meanings and sentences) with the class
- Choosing a word – explaining to the class

Background Information

This lesson gives students the opportunity to practice using a dictionary. The teacher must first explain how to use a dictionary; for example, looking at the top of the page, how to pronounce words, different uses for a word.

For example:

Pronunciation, with the accent on the first part of the word.

This is the adverb.

hideous (hid-ee-uss) *adj* ugly, revolting. **hideously** *adv*

It is an adjective or describing word.

The new statue on the square is hideous!

Sometimes there is an example of how the word is used in a sentence.

Before the Lesson

The teacher must have a list of things he/she wants to show the class about using a dictionary.

All students must have a dictionary.

Students will be working in pairs.

The Lesson (Pages 65 and 66)

The teacher explains how to use a dictionary, and students must look up some interesting words that the teacher gives.

Students work in pairs, using their dictionaries to match words and pictures.

Students look up meanings of words given, discuss them with their partner, and use them in sentences of their own.

Students draw pictures to show the meanings of the given words.

Students discuss all the words with the rest of the class, giving meanings and using the words in sentences.

Students choose a word from the dictionary (a word they are not familiar with). They must see if the class knows the meaning. They must explain the meaning of the word to the class.

Answers

1. (a) belfry – part of a tower where the bell hangs
    (b) mull – to think
    (c) cherub – angel
    (d) char – burn
2. Answers (sentences) will vary, but meanings of words are:
    (a) superb – excellent
    (b) lilac – light purple
    (c) cordial – pleasant/friendly **or** drink which needs diluting with water before being drunk
    (d) lax – not strict
    (e) crib – a baby's bed
    (f) dinghy – type of boat
    (g) woozy – dizzy, unwell
    (h) fuse – to mix together
    (i) gripe – complain (informal)
3. (a) tutu – type of skirt worn by ballerinas
    (b) garb – clothing
    (c) shallot – kind of small onion
4.–5. Teacher check

Additional Activities

Students can make sentences with a list of more challenging words given by the teacher.

Students can play a dictionary game, whereby the teacher gives a word to the class and they must look it up as quickly as they can. One student gets selected to write the meaning on the board. Other students say if he/she is correct.

Students can display new words in the classroom.

Students can look at websites with interesting words.

The teacher can use all new words learned in a paragraph that the students must then explain in their own words.

The teacher can discuss new words in our language, such as computer terms or words like "envirocrime" (crime against the environment).

Look It Up!

1 Match up the words and pictures.

Make sure you have your dictionary for this lesson.

(a) belfry

(b) mull

(c) cherub

(d) char

2 Look up these words in the dictionary. Discuss their meanings with your partner. Write a sentence using each word.

(a) superb _____

_____

_____

(b) lilac _____

_____

_____

(c) cordial _____

_____

_____

(d) lax _____

_____

_____

(e) crib _____

_____

_____

(f) dinghy _____

_____

_____

(g) woozy _____

_____

_____

(h) fuse _____

_____

_____

Did you know?

"Bovine" means to do with cows. It can also mean rather slow and stupid! Hmph!

(i) gripe _____

_____

_____

Look It Up!

3 Draw pictures to show the meaning of these words.

tutu	garb	shallot

4 (a) Discuss the meanings of the words above with your class.

(b) Use each word in a sentence.

(c) Is anyone able to use all three words in one sentence?

Write the sentence here.

_____

_____

5 Open your dictionary at any page and choose a difficult word. (Go to the next page if you need to.)

(a) What word did you choose?

_____

(b) Meaning of word:

_____

_____

_____

_____

Add all new words to your wordbook!

(c) See if the rest of your class knows what it means. Give the class the correct meaning!

DESIGN A CREST

Objective: Experience varied and consistent oral language activity as a preparation for other activities.

Activities Covered

- Discussing crests and meanings of colors and symbols
- Discussing what the class/school stands for, what aims are, strengths, etc.
- Drawing a rough draft of crest
- Discussing student's crests
- Drawing and labeling final crest
- Evaluating final crest

Background Information

Oral language will almost always precede writing activities; this lesson demonstrates how oral language has an impact on the final activity.

Before the Lesson

The teacher should access information about crests and what the different colors and symbols stand for. This information must be discussed with the class before the students make the rough draft of their crest.

A suitable website is: *www.fleurdelis.com/meanings.htm* (It can get very complicated so it is best to stick to the basics and choose only a few colors and symbols.)

The Lesson (Pages 68 and 69)

The teacher discusses with the class examples of crests and the meaning of symbols and colors. (Basic meanings, it needn't be too in depth.)

The class discusses what the class/school stands for (depending on who the crest is for). In doing this, students can decide what the aims are, what the strengths and interests are, what is important to them, their values, etc.

Students draw a rough draft of what they think the crest should look like and label it to show why they have chosen specific colors/symbols.

Students show and discuss their crests with the class and the class must decide what the final crest should entail. (Hopefully, different ideas can be taken from different students.)

Students draw the final crest, with labels.

The crest can be displayed for the rest of the school, and the other classes can give feedback. Perhaps a suggestion box can be introduced if it is a school crest, and the class can discuss the suggestions and see if there is anything they would change.

Answers

1.–7. Teacher check

Additional Activities

Students can design a crest/badge that represents themselves.

Students can look at family crests (particularly their own) and make up their own family crest, after having had a class discussion.

The class can have a discussion on families. Students can then discuss their own families and describe them to the class. Then students can make a family tree to be displayed in the classroom.

Design a Crest

We are going to design a crest for your school.
If your school already has one, then you can design a
crest for your own class.

(1) I am going to use the following colors and symbols on my crest:

colors	symbols

(2) Draw what you think the crest should look like. Label it to show what your colors and symbols mean.

*Your crest should show what
your school/class stands for.*

(3) Show your crest to your
class and explain it.

Design a Crest

4 Decide as a class what the final crest should have on it and look like.

5 Draw the crest below and label it to show what the different colors and symbols stand for.

Get comments from the rest of the school!

6 Do you like the final crest?   yes   no

7 Is there anything you would change about it and why?

_____

_____

_____

MORE INFORMATION NEEDED!

Objective: Learn to use questions as a mechanism for expanding and developing a story.

Activities Covered

- Reading a passage
- Answer questions to plan a story
- Writing a story using prompt
- Reading a story to the class
- Assessing the class's opinions

Background Information

This lesson allows students to use questions to extend the story. This lesson can be repeated so the students get used to asking themselves questions and elaborating on details. Students can use the same questions when they are writing a story, letter, paragraph, etc. The "question" words can be displayed in the classroom.

Before the Lesson

The teacher can show the gist of the lesson by giving an example of a story similar to that on the sheet (see *Answers*).

The Lesson (Pages 71 and 72)

The teacher gives an example of the paragraph and the students must ask questions to expand on it.

Students read a paragraph on their worksheet.

Students discuss and write answers to the given questions.

Students rewrite the story, adding the new details.

Students read their story to the class.

Students assess what the class thought of their story.

Answers

1. Answers will vary. Here is an example of some answers:
   (a) Tom went with his friend, James.
   (b) They went to a run-down house.
   (c) They went there to explore.
   (d) It happened on Friday after school.
   (e) They were exploring the old house and when they went up the stairs, the stairs broke and Tom was hurt.

2. Example:
   On Friday after school, James asked Tom to go with him to an old house in the town. Nobody lived there any more and the house was falling apart. Tom knew in his heart that he should not go along. His parents had often warned him to stay away from old houses and buildings. James said it was a great place to explore and assured Tom they would be very careful. They arrived at the house and explored around outside, but that got boring so James suggested they take a peek inside. The front door was open and the two of them carefully walked in. Tom was very afraid because he could hardly see a thing and there was a funny damp smell. It felt like a haunted house. They could just make out the staircase, and James went ahead to climb it. Tom warned him that it could be dangerous, but James said he was only going halfway up. Tom thought he'd better follow, otherwise he might look like a coward. The stairs creaked under their weight. On the seventh stair, Tom could feel the wood beneath his feet give way. The staircase literally fell apart and Tom fell to the ground. James landed on top of him and so did a pile of wood. James got up and tried to help Tom up, but Tom could not stand. James had to run home to get help and leave poor Tom there, crying in pain in the old, dusty house. Tom was rushed to the hospital and X-rays showed he had badly fractured his leg. James felt very guilty about the incident, and he and Tom are more sensible now!

3.–4. Teacher check

Additional Activities

The teacher can give the class just one sentence of a story starter. Students can come up with the rest of the story by asking questions. This can be done orally and the teacher can write the story on the board.

Students can write their stories using a word processing program and print out their work for display.

Students can retell well-known stories and decide how the basic questions have been answered.

Students can read poetry and see how the basic questions have been answered. (how, which, what, when, why, etc).

More Information Needed!

We are going to make our story longer by asking questions and adding more details.

Read this passage.

> One day, Tom got into serious trouble. He knew his friend was wrong when he suggested it, but Tom went along with him anyway. He knew in his heart that he shouldn't have gone. Now it was too late.

1 We are going to add to the passage to make a story. First we need to make up answers to these questions.

(a) **Who** did Tom go with?

_____

(b) **Where** did they go?

_____

_____

_____

_____

_____

WHAT?
WHERE?
WHEN?
WHO?
WHY?

(c) **Why** did they go there?

_____

_____

(d) **When** did this happen?

_____

_____

(e) **What** happened?

_____

_____

More Information Needed!

2 Write the story, adding the new details.

_____

_____

_____

_____

_____

_____

_____

_____

_____

_____

_____

_____

_____

_____

_____

_____

_____

_____

_____

_____

_____

3 (a) Read your story to the class.

(b) What did the class think of your story? very good good fair

4 How could you improve your story?

_____

_____

_____

_____

WHERE'S THE PERIOD?

Objective: Learn to use a wider range of punctuation marks with greater accuracy as part of the revision and editing process.

Activities Covered

- Naming punctuation marks and explaining when they are used
- **Pair Work –** showing punctuation with hand signals
- Filling in correct punctuation in sentences and in a poem
- Using punctuation marks in own sentences
- Reading sentences to the class

Background Information

This is mostly meant to be a fun and informal lesson which can precede more serious lessons to do with punctuation. Students need to be given much practice in using punctuation and constantly need to be corrected when punctuation marks are used incorrectly. Students need to be aware of the importance of correct punctuation, so the teacher should show them many examples of correct and incorrect punctuation. This lesson deals only with the period, comma, apostrophe (contractions), exclamation mark and question mark, as well as capital letters. More punctuation marks can be dealt with once the students have had plenty of practice with these basics.

Before the Lesson

The class will be divided into pairs.

The teacher should have examples for students to do together as a class. (Adding punctuation to simple sentences, including capital letters.)

The teacher should show students how hand signals for punctuation could work (showing a comma, question mark, etc., in the air with a finger).

The Lesson (Pages 74 and 75)

Students name punctuation marks and when they are used. Teacher draws punctuation marks on the board.

Pair Work – Students read the sentences aloud, taking turns, and show where punctuation marks should go by using hand signals. Students correct each other where necessary.

Students rewrite the sentences using correct punctuation.

Students add suitable punctuation to the poem to make it easier to read.

Still in pairs, students write sentences using each of the given punctuation marks.

Students read some of their sentences to the class, showing punctuation marks with hand signals.

Answers

1.–2. (a) Get off the grass!
   (b) Can Jim stay over tonight?
   (c) For dinner I would like carrots, cabbage, broccoli, peas and corn.
   (d) Look out! There's a lion behind you!
   (e) I can't wait to visit Paris to see the Eiffel Tower.
   (f) Where will we place the Christmas tree?
   (g) Sir, can we please have English, math and science for homework?
   (h) My birthday is in June and I hope I get books, pens, chocolate and money.

3. Answers will vary – accept any that use punctuation correctly. Here is an example:

> *Tricks*
>
> Mom, today I saw geese that were colored bright red!
> Oh, please stop talking nonsense, Fred!
>
> Mom, today I saw monkeys about to wed!
> Oh, do stop telling such fibs now, Fred!
>
> Mom, today I saw a man nearly stab a woman dead!
> Oh, I do wish you'd stop all your lying, Fred!
>
> Mom, today I saw an elephant pulling a sled!
> Oh, do tell the truth for once, dear Fred!
>
> Mom, today I saw a man with a donkey head!
> I'm tired of all your rubbish, now go to bed, Fred!
>
> Then Mom looked out the window,
> and what did she see there?
> But people dressed quite strangely,
> and animals quite rare.
> They were practicing their acts and stunts,
> parading up and down.
> Poor Fred was only telling Mom
> the circus was in town!

4.–5.   Teacher check

Additional Activities

The teacher could point out to students that our voices tell when there is a period, comma, exclamation mark and question mark. Students can practice reading aloud sentences with these punctuation marks.

Students can read poetry—some with punctuation and some without any at all—and see the effects.

Where's the Period?

1 With your partner, take turns to read the sentences below. Punctuate the sentences, using hand signals, as the sentence is being read. Correct each other where necessary!

> Can you name some punctuation marks?

(a) get off the grass

_____

_____

(b) can jim stay over tonight

_____

_____

(c) for dinner i would like carrots cabbage broccoli peas and corn

_____

_____

_____

_____

(d) look out there's a lion behind you

_____

_____

(e) i cannot wait to visit paris to see the eiffel tower

_____

_____

_____

(f) where will we place the christmas tree

_____

_____

(g) sir can we please have english maths and science for homework

_____

_____

(h) my birthday is in june and i hope i get books pens chocolate and money

_____

_____

2 (a) Write the sentences above correctly, using the following punctuation.

(periods)　(question marks)　(apostrophes)

(commas)　(exclamation marks)　(capital letters)

(b) Discuss your answers with your class. Correct any you got wrong.

(c) How many did you get right out of eight? ☐

Where's the Period?

③ (a) With your partner, try to read this poem. It is quite difficult, as it has no punctuation.

(b) Add punctuation to the poem. Try reading the poem again. Punctuation should make it easier to read.

> ### Tricks
>
> Mom today I saw geese that were colored bright red
> Oh please stop talking nonsense Fred
>
> Mom today I saw monkeys about to wed
> Oh do stop telling such fibs now Fred
>
> Mom today I saw a man nearly stab a woman dead
> Oh I do wish you'd stop all your lying Fred
>
> Mom today I saw an elephant pulling a sled
> Oh do tell the truth for once dear Fred
>
> Mom today I saw a man with a donkey head
> I'm tired of all your rubbish now go to bed Fred
>
>
>
> Then Mom looked out the window
> and what did she see there
> But people dressed quite strangely
> and animals quite rare
> They were practicing their acts and stunts
> parading up and down
> Poor Fred was only telling Mom
> the circus was in town

④ Still in pairs, use each of these punctuation marks in a sentence.

! _____

. _____

, _____

? _____

Without punctuation, reading wouldn't make sense!

⑤ Read some of your sentences to the class. Use hand signals as you read them!

ALL ABOUT YOUR LIFE

Objective: Discuss issues that directly affect his/her life.

Activities Covered

- Answering questions anonymously
- Class discussion on class's answers

Background Information

This lesson focuses on discussion. Students fill in a sheet anonymously so that they can answer the questions completely honestly without worrying about what other people may think. The teacher should approach this lesson in a sensitive manner. He/she should be aware of students' feelings and reactions and encourage students to do the same.

Before the Lesson

The teacher can have other points of discussion ready about what affects students' lives.

The Lesson (Pages 77 and 78)

Students fill in the questionnaire anonymously.

Students hand in their sheet and the teacher discusses the questions with the class, reading out several answers and ideas that the students have given. Names must not be used.

The teacher can write headings on the board with various ideas underneath, just to sum the lesson up. This can be done during the lesson as discussion takes place.

Answers

Answers will vary.

Additional Activities

Students can come up with their own ideas about what affects them in their everyday lives; for example, meals, bedtimes, interests, friends, teachers, moving, death in a family, divorce, siblings.

The class can do a project on *What Affects Us* and this can be displayed for the school. Students can use pictures, song lyrics, display of books, paragraphs, photos, foodstuffs, etc.

Students can read and discuss poetry that concerns issues that affect them; for example:

> *Discarded*
>
> A minute ago, we were friends to the end.
> Now I seem to be driving you around the bend.
> What did I do or what did I say?
> How did I make you feel this way?
> I told you my secrets, you know it all.
> I'm there for you always, whenever you call.
> I don't understand it – please explain how
> You can suddenly hate me and torture me now!
> I'll be here waiting, interested to hear,
> Why now I am nothing, when you held me so dear.

All About Your Life

This sheet can be filled in anonymously. That means you do not need to write your name on it.

Be truthful with your answers!

1 Answer these questions.

THINGS THAT AFFECT YOUR LIFE

(a) What is the best thing about school? _____

_____

(b) What is the worst thing about school? _____

_____

(c) What would you change about school if you could? _____

_____

(d) What is your favorite subject? _____

(e) What is your least favorite subject? _____

(f) What is the best thing about your home life? _____

_____

_____

(g) What is the worst thing about your home life? _____

_____

_____

(h) What at home irritates you the most? _____

_____

(i) Do you get along with all your family members?   yes   no

Explain. _____   sometimes

_____

All About Your Life

THINGS THAT AFFECT YOUR LIFE

(j) Do you have good friends? | yes | no | sometimes |

Explain. _____

_____

(k) What things do you like doing with your friends? _____

_____

_____

(l) What makes you worried? _____

_____

_____

(m) What makes you happy? _____

_____

_____

(n) What interests do you have? _____

_____

_____

_____

(o) Who could you speak to if you had a problem? _____

_____

_____

(2) Which three questions did you find the most difficult to answer?

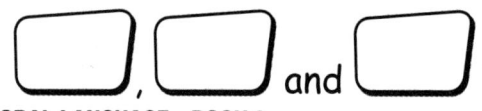

(3) Hand your sheet to your teacher. The teacher will discuss all the different answers with your class. But don't worry! No one will know the answers you gave!

HAPPY ENDINGS?

Objective: Discuss a story being read and predict future endings and likely outcomes in it.

Activities Covered

- Writing an ending to a given story beginning
- Reading the story ending to the class or group
- **Group Work –** making up endings to a well-known fairytale
- Reading endings to the class
- Voting for the best ending

Background Information

Students have to have a solid understanding of the storyline before they can predict a likely ending. For this reason, students are asked to think of a fairy tale and propose possible endings. The teacher can get students thinking along these lines with a discussion; for example, "What do you think happened to Sleeping Beauty and her prince? Where did they go? Where did they live?" "Did Goldilocks ever go walking on her own again? Did she ever encounter the bears again, and if so, what did she say to them?"

Before the Lesson

The teacher can have examples of fairy tales where the endings can be changed or expanded.

Students will be divided into groups.

The Lesson (Pages 80 and 81)

The teacher reads the short given passage to the class.

Students write a possible ending.

Students discuss their endings and read them to their class or group.

Group Work – Students make up two possible endings for a common fairy tale.

Students read their endings to the class.

The class votes for the best ending.

Students write the best ending on their sheet.

Answers

1.–3.   Stories will vary, but could include the following explanations: *Bridget was having a dream./Bridget had lost her memory./ Bridget's parents had brought her to this place while she was asleep./Bridget had been very ill and was brought to this place to recuperate./Bridget had been kidnapped.*

4.   Teacher check

Additional Activities

The teacher can read short stories to the class and students can predict the most likely outcome. The teacher then reads the ending.

Students can watch TV programs (children's programs with a storyline) that the teacher has taped. Halfway through, students predict a likely ending, and then continue to watch the tape to see the ending. The teacher can discuss the differences between the real ending and the predicted endings.

Happy Endings?

And they lived happily ever after.

(1) Read this passage.

One day, Bridget woke up at the usual time. When she looked out the window, she saw a beach, the sea and a blue sunny sky — but they didn't live anywhere near the beach! Where was she, and how did she get here? Bridget heard her family talking downstairs and they were all talking normally. Her favorite shoes were next to the bed and her clothes were strewn on the floor, which was very normal! Bridget could smell delicious pancakes and her tummy started to grumble. She got out of bed and walked with hesitation down the stairs. Nothing in this house looked familiar. She found her way to the kitchen.

"Good morning, dear, would you like some pancakes?" said Bridget's mom cheerfully.

"What is going on, Mom? Where are we?"

"What ever do you mean, dear?"

(2) Complete the story.

_____

_____

_____

_____

_____

_____

_____

_____

_____

_____

(3) Read your story ending to your class or group.

Happy Endings?

④ Work as a group. Choose a well-known fairy tale and write two alternative endings for it.

(a) Which fairy tale did you chose?

_____

_____

(b) Ending number 1:

_____

_____

_____

_____

_____

_____

_____

_____

_____

_____

_____

(c) Ending number 2:

_____

_____

_____

_____

_____

_____

_____

_____

_____

_____

_____

_____

The ending is often the most important part of the story!

(d) Have a class vote for the best ending. Write the ending here. (If it's one of your endings, circle it.)

_____

_____

_____

_____

CAN YOU HELP?

Objective: Discuss different possible solutions to a problem.

Activities Covered

- Class discussion
- Thinking of possible solutions to common problems
- **Group Work –** solving given problem
- Choosing correct answer

Background Information

The objective here has been taken quite literally, with a discussion about common problems students may have. Much discussion needs to take place so that solutions to the problems are found through weighing up all the possibilities.

Before the Lesson

The teacher can have a list of common problems that can be discussed with the class.

The class will be divided into groups.

The Lesson (Pages 83 and 79)

As a class, the students read the given problems and discuss them one by one. Students must give their ideas as to how the problem can be solved, and the class can come to an agreement as to the best possible solution. Students write a solution for each problem.

The teacher can then discuss with the class other problems students may have. At this point, the teacher could explain what *Kids Help Line* is all about.

Group Work – Each group is given a particular problem and the group must discuss the problem and how it can be solved. Some problems are suggested in *Answers*.

The groups must present their problem and solution to the class, who must comment on the solution.

Students must choose the correct statement regarding what they should do if they have a problem.

Answers

1. Answers will vary, but possible solutions might include:
   (a) The student should discuss his/her concerns with the parents, and tell them how it makes him/her feel./The student should approach a trusted adult and explain his/her feelings to that person.

   (b) Perhaps a different kind of pet would not make the sister sick, such as an animal without fur, like a bird or hairless cat!
   (c) The student should approach his/her teacher at a quiet time, perhaps after school, and tell the teacher the difficulties he/she is experiencing./The student should tell his/her parents about the student's difficulties in math, and the parents can perhaps get extra math lessons for the student and/or approach his/her teacher.
   (d) The student should try to make friends with others and not show concern over the fact that the other friend abandoned him or her. (Hard to do!)

2. Possible problems that can be given to the groups:

   My brother/sister keeps coming into my room without asking and fiddling with my stuff.

   I know that my friend is stealing from the store, but I don't want to get him/her into trouble.

   I have the most awful clothes, and I am embarrassed to go out wearing them. My parents say clothes are not important.

   Every Sunday, our family visits our aunt and we spend all day there. It is so boring, and I have nothing to do there because she does not even have a TV. My aunt is quite nice, but I wish I didn't have to go there any more.

   I know that someone in my class is being bullied, but I don't want to tell, in case I start getting bullied too.

3. Talk to someone you can trust.

Additional Activities

Students can look at real problem pages found in newspapers and magazines and discuss them as a class. (The teacher should check the content first!)

Can You Help?

We all have problems of some sort. Nobody's life is perfect.

1 Discuss these problems and figure out some possible solutions.

PROBLEMS: **SOLUTIONS:**

(a) My parents are always arguing and it drives me crazy! They seem to fight over the smallest things!

_____
_____
_____
_____

(b) I wish I could get a dog. I have wanted a pet for so long but my sister is allergic to animal fur.

_____
_____
_____
_____

(c) I am really struggling with math; I just don't seem to get it. Every day I dread the math lesson, and I don't know what to do!

_____
_____
_____
_____

(d) My best friend has joined another group of friends and is now ignoring me completely. I don't have other friends and I feel so hurt and alone.

_____
_____
_____
_____

Did you know that you can phone organizations that help children with their problems? Find the name and number of an organization like this.

Can You Help?

PANIC BUTTON

2 In your group, discuss the problem your teacher has given you.

(a) What is the problem?

_____

_____

_____

_____

(b) How did your group think the problem could be solved?

_____

_____

_____

_____

_____

_____

_____

_____

_____

(c) What did your class think of your solution?

1 2 3 4 5

A problem shared is a problem halved.

3 Color in the best thing to do if you have a problem.

Don't think about it and it will go away.

Keep your problem a secret.

Talk to someone you can trust.

Try to solve the problem on your own.

HOW MUCH DO YOU KNOW?

Objective: Discuss what he/she knows of a particular topic or process as a basis for encountering new concepts.

Activities Covered

- Answering questions
- Discussing answers in class
- Researching
- Drawing a picture

Background Information

The idea of this lesson is that students will gain more information on something they are already familiar with. They can add to their knowledge through research and discussion. Students can sometimes come to see a particular topic in a different light.

Before the Lesson

Students will need to be given time to do their research.

Teachers can have prepared information about kookaburras.

Students will need reference material, including illustrations, about kookaburras.

The Lesson (Pages 86 and 87)

Students answer the first five questions and discuss the answers as a class.

Students attempt the next five questions and have another class discussion. Students can help each other out with the answers.

Students research the next five questions and draw a picture of a kookaburra.

The last five questions are discussed.

The topic is discussed in its entirety.

Answers

1. (a) bird (b) medium
   (c) yes (d) brown and white
   (e) feathers
2. Teacher check
3. (a) large insects/lizards/snakes/small mammals/frogs/fish
   (b) no (c) unfriendly
   (d) no (e) 13–20 years
4. Teacher check
5. (a) Perches on a branch or wire and waits patiently for prey to pass by.
   (b) 2–4
   (c) Boisterous "laugh"—kook-kook-kook-ka-ka-ka—cackle.
   (d) *Dacelo gaudichaud (or leachii/novaegunieae/tyro)*
   (e) no
6. Answers will vary
7.–8. Teacher check

Additional Activities

The same lesson can be done with almost any topic of which the students have some knowledge. The teacher should start with the very basics and go on to more challenging aspects of the topic. As well as learning more about the particular topic, it will hopefully broaden students' horizons, so that they may view the topic differently.

How Much Do You Know?

1 Color the correct answers to these questions.

The questions in this lesson get more and more difficult!

(a) What is a kookaburra?

mammal   reptile   bird   insect

(b) Is it large, medium, or small?

large   medium   small

(c) Can it fly?

yes   no

(d) What colors is it?

brown and white   green and white   red and white   purple and white   black and white

(e) What body covering does it have?

fur   scales   feathers

2 Discuss your answers with the class.

3 Now, the questions get a bit harder! See if you can answer each question in a sentence.

(a) Name one thing that a kookaburra eats. _____

_____

(b) Does it have a hooked beak like a parrot? _____

_____

(c) Is it a friendly or unfriendly bird? _____

_____

(d) Is it nocturnal? _____

_____

(e) What is its maximum life span? _____

_____

4 Discuss your answers with the class.

Did you know?
Kookaburras can prey on snakes up to three feet in length!

How Much Do You Know?

5 Now, even harder! You may have to do some research to answer these questions. Answer each in a sentence.

(a) How does a kookaburra hunt for its prey?

_____

_____

(b) How many eggs does a kookaburra lay? _____

_____

(c) Describe its call. _____

_____

(d) What is its scientific name? _____

(e) Does it migrate to warmer climates during the winter?

_____

6 Write one other interesting fact you have discovered about kookaburras.

_____

_____

7 Use reference materials to draw a picture of a kookaburra.

8 Once all the questions have been answered, have a class discussion on all you know about the kookaburra.

WHAT WOULD HAPPEN IF ...?

Objective: Discuss causes and effects in relation to processes and events and predict possible outcomes.

Activities Covered

- Answering and discussing "what if" questions
- Reading a news story and retelling it verbally to a partner
- Answering questions
- Choosing a news story of the week
- Answering the same questions

Background Information

This lesson should begin with a general discussion about causes and effects in our everyday lives. For example, when we talk in class (cause) we may get into trouble (effect)/If we work really hard on a project (cause), we will get a good grade (effect), etc. The main focus of the lesson should be discussion.

Before the Lesson

The teacher can have examples of "cause and effect" situations in our everyday lives. Students do not need to learn these terms, but must understand their meaning.

Students will need to choose a news story of the week before the lesson. Students must look at newspapers or watch the news (international and local); this could be given for homework the night before.

Students will need to work with a partner.

The Lesson (Pages 89 and 90)

The teacher discusses "cause" and "effect" with the class.

Students answer "what if" questions and discuss them with the class.

Students read the news story given.

Students answer the questions.

Students discuss their answers to Question 5 with the class, mentioning the causes and effects.

Some students tell the class their news story.

Students answer the questions orally, as a class.

Answers

1. Answers will vary, but could include:
   (a) You would be smelly and have germs.
   (b) Your parents would say "thank you."
   (c) You would be unhealthy and could get sick.
   (d) Your teacher would get angry./You might have to stay in at break time.
   (e) The student would be grateful and would think you were a good friend.
   (f) Your teacher might say "Well done" or "Good answer."
   (g) The shopkeeper would be very angry./The shopkeeper might tell your parents./The shopkeeper might call the police.
   (h) You would not find a very well paid job./The job might be too difficult for you./You would not have enough of an education.
2.–4. Teacher check
5. (a) The story was about a fire that broke out in a house.
   (b) An unattended fire caused it.
   (c) The family could have been trapped inside./If they had smoke alarms, they would have been aware of the fire much more quickly.
   (d) The family may have to seek other accommodation while their house is being repaired. I think they will be careful in the future.
6. Teacher check

Additional Activities

Students can discuss well-known legends and talk about the events in the story, what the effects were, and what might have happened afterwards.

What Would Happen If ...?

1 Work with a partner to discuss and answer what would happen if ...

(a) you never bathed or showered?

_____

_____

_____

(b) you washed the dishes every day for a week?

_____

_____

_____

(c) you ate only junk food?

_____

_____

_____

(d) you never did your homework?

_____

_____

_____

(e) you helped someone in your class who was stuck with his/her work?

_____

_____

_____

(f) you answered a question correctly in class?

_____

_____

_____

(g) you took a chocolate bar from a store without paying for it?

_____

_____

_____

(h) you left school now to go to work?

_____

_____

_____

2 Discuss your answers with the class. Color whether your class mostly agreed or disagreed with your answers.

agreed   disagreed

What Would Happen If ...?

3 Read this news story with your partner.

On Friday morning, a fire crew was called to Church Street to put out a fire. It was 2 a.m. and the family inside, consisting of a mother, father and two sons under the age of five, managed to escape the blazing building. Another survivor was Rusty, their quick-thinking Labrador, who had alerted the whole family by barking loudly. After careful investigation, it is believed that an unattended fire in the living room had sent sparks out, causing the furniture to catch fire. There was no fire screen and the house was not equipped with smoke alarms.

4 Take turns to retell the story to your partner in your own words.

5 Answer these questions about the news story.

(a) What is the news story about? _____

_____

(b) What caused it to happen? _____

_____

(c) How could it have happened differently? _____

_____

_____

_____

(d) What do you think will happen now? _____

_____

_____

_____

6 Choose a news story of the week and answer the same questions for the story as above. Bring newspaper clippings to school if you can. Discuss your answers with the class.

What sort of effect does it have on your teacher when you don't do your homework?

ASK AWAY!

Objective: *Listen to a presentation and discuss and decide which are the important questions to ask.*

Objective: *Learn how to use the basic key questions.*

Activities Covered

- Discussing process of making potato chips
- Answering questions
- Choosing the most important questions
- Reading rhyme
- Devising questions on given rhyme

Background Information

This lesson encompasses two main objectives, both on asking questions. Students should be reminded how we start and end questions. There are many different types of lessons that would incorporate these objectives. The teacher could simply read a story and get students to ask relevant questions, or students could look at advertising and ask questions about the product. These objectives could be covered when students are learning other subjects, with students asking important questions about the topic that has been learned. Students should always be encouraged to ask questions and should be told that if they are unsure about something, they should ask! This does not only apply to school.

Before the Lesson

The teacher can have examples of how we start and end questions and different situations in life where it is necessary to ask important questions. Students will work in groups.

The Lesson (Pages 92 and 93)

The teacher must remind students how questions are started and ended. Perhaps the words "which, why, when, where, who, what" can be written on the board.

The teacher reads through the process of making potato chips with the students.

Students discuss the process and answer Questions 2 (a)–(j) verbally, in their group.

Students choose the five most important questions about the process of making potato chips. (Not other aspects!)

Students read an advertisement and make up questions, using prompts.

Students discuss their answers for Question 4 with the rest of the class.

The class could come up with original ideas to answer their own questions about the advertisement.

Answers

1.–2. Teacher check
3. (a), (b), (d), (e) and (i)
4. Answers will vary, but could include:
   (a) Why are there age restrictions on the potato chips?
   (b) When did they come out?
   (c) Who were the potato chips named after?
   (d) What are the different flavors?
   (e) Where can I buy them?

Additional Activities

Pair Work – Students must ask their partners appropriate questions to find out about their weekend.

Students can read nursery rhymes and ask questions. Then they can make up the answers.

The teacher can read a paragraph, poem, or short story to the class and students must ask relevant questions.

Ask Away!

(1) Read and look at the information below.

How potato chips are made:

The potatoes are washed and checked. Damaged potatoes are removed.

The potatoes are washed and peeled.

The potatoes are sliced and washed again.

The slices are fried and flavoring is added.

Samples are checked and tested to make sure the quality is right.

The packaging process takes place.

Bags are stamped with a "best before" date and a code which gives information about when and where they were made.

The potato chips are on their way to the stores.

Ask Away!

2 Discuss the answers to the questions with your group.

> (a) When is the flavoring added?
>
> (b) What happens after the potatoes are peeled?
>
> (c) What kind of trucks are used to transport the chips?
>
> (d) Are the damaged potatoes removed?
>
> (e) Why are the samples checked?
>
> (f) Who enjoys eating chips?
>
> (g) What color is the "Salt and Vinegar" bag?
>
> (h) How many chips are in one bag?
>
> (i) How many times are the potatoes washed?
>
> (j) What should one do if one buys "out of date" chips?

3 Use a colored crayon to circle what you think are the five most important questions about the process of making potato chips.

*Remember!
Only questions about the **process** are important here.*

4 Look at this advertisement.

Write five questions you could ask about the product.

Catherine's chips

In 5 super hot flavors!

Munch and crunch them for lunch!

Not suitable for children under the age of 10.

(a) Why _____

_____

(b) When _____

_____

(c) Who _____

_____

(d) What _____

_____

(e) Where _____

_____

WHAT INTERESTS YOU?

Objective: *Make presentations to the class about his/her own particular interests.*

Activities Covered

- Writing possible interests for different occupations
- Writing down own interests
- Telling class about own interests
- Assessing own talk
- Listening to other class members talk about their interests
- Taking notes

Background Information

This lesson will allow students to present their own personal interests to the class. The class must sit and listen quietly and must have respect for the interests of others. Perhaps the lesson could be started with a discussion about different interests people have, as the students may not be aware of their own interests!

Before the Lesson

The teacher could have a list of interests, common and uncommon.

The Lesson (Pages 95 and 96)

Students write down possible interests for the given occupations and occupations of their own choice.

Students write down their own interests.

Students tell the class about their interests.

Students assess their talk.

Students listen to other class members talk about their interests. While doing this, they take notes of each class member's talk.

Answers

1. Answers will vary, but could include:
   (a) nurse – people, helping others, medicine, healing, human body, health
   (b) chef – food, cooking, restaurants
   (c) teacher – children, learning, helping others
   (d) archaeologist – ancient objects, history, buried treasure
   (e) carpenter – wood, furniture, carving
   (f) soldier – war, fighting for own country, weapons, helping others
   (g) chiropodist – feet, healing, making others feel better
   (h) architect – buildings, plans, building materials, design
   (i) secretary – paperwork, filing, computers, people, bookkeeping
2.–4. Teacher check

Additional Activities

Students can tell the class about their favorite things; for example, game, day of the week, chips, subject, sport, book.

Students can read poems about other students' interests.

Students can look at students from other countries and how their interests may differ from their own.

Students could make a display of their interests in the classroom.

What Interests You?

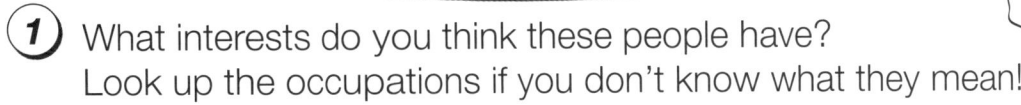

We are all interested in something. For some of you, it may even be school!

1 What interests do you think these people have?
Look up the occupations if you don't know what they mean!

| (a) Nurse  | (b) Chef  | (c) Teacher  |

(d) Archaeologist _____

(e) Carpenter _____

(f) Soldier _____

(g) Chiropodist _____

(h) Architect _____

(i) Secretary _____

2 Choose three different occupations. Draw a person doing each job. Write what interests you think each has.

| (a) _____ | (b) _____ | (c) _____ |

What Interests You?

Your interests make you interesting!

3 What are your interests?

(a) Write your ideas in the box below and tell the class about your interests.

(b) How did your talk go? | Awesome! | | OK! | | Awful! |

(c) Why? _____

_____

_____

4 Listen to the other students in your class talk about their interests. Choose one student. Write his/her name. Write notes about the student's interests as you listen to his/her talk.

Name of student: _____

Interests:

WHAT DO YOU LIKE?

Objective: Justify personal likes and dislikes.

Activities Covered

- Deciding if they like or dislike things listed, justifying their answers
- Writing what they like or dislike, using headings
- **Group Work** – discussing their likes and dislikes, justifying them

Background Information

This lesson gives students the opportunity to tell others the things they like and dislike. The teacher must tell the students that they have to justify their opinions. For example, it is not enough to say "I hate peas" but rather "I hate peas because they feel all mushy in my mouth."

Before the Lesson

The class will be divided into pairs and then groups.

The Lesson (Pages 98 and 99)

The class can have a brief discussion on their likes and dislikes, using topics not already covered in the lesson; for example, subjects at school, other aspects about school.

Students read a list of things and check whether they like or dislike them.

Students compare their likes and dislikes to those of their partner,and give some justification for their likes and dislikes.

Students write their likes and dislikes under headings.

Group Work – Students describe their likes and dislikes to the group, each taking a turn to speak. Students must justify why they like or dislike something.

Answers

Teacher check

Additional Activities

The teacher can discuss with the class different phobias (strong dislikes) people have; for example, didaskaleinophobia – fear of going to school, arachnophobia – fear of spiders. Look at website: *www.phobialist.com* (for teacher only – interesting words!).

Each student in the class can bring something that he/she likes to school; for example, food item, a photo, book, picture. These can be displayed in the classroom under a heading "Things We Like."

Students can read poems about the likes and dislikes of other people.

What Do You Like?

I like students! (They're tasty!)

The things that we like and dislike are part of who we are. We all have our personal tastes.

1 Working with a partner, look at the following list. Check whether you and your partner like or dislike the items on the list.

	Me		My partner	
	Like	Dislike	Like	Dislike
(a) carrots				
(b) motorcycles				
(c) strawberry jam				
(d) bunk beds				
(e) popcorn				
(f) haircuts				
(g) ballet				
(h) swimming				
(i) bowling				
(j) computers				
(k) reading				
(l) rainy weather				
(m) toast				
(n) dogs				

2 (a) How many "likes" do you have?

(b) How many "dislikes" do you have?

(c) Do you always like the same things as your partner?

(d) Which item do you like the most? _____

Why? _____

(e) Which item do you dislike the most? _____

Why? _____

What Do You Like?

3 Write in the tables below what you like and dislike.

	I like	I dislike
(a) color		
(b) TV program		
(c) type of clothing		
(d) sport		
(e) type of food		
(f) activity		
(g) pet		
(h) type of drink		
(i) store		
(j) toy		

I also like _____

_____

_____

_____

_____

_____

I also dislike _____

_____

_____

_____

_____

_____

4 Tell your group about your likes and dislikes and why you like or dislike these things.

It's not good to dislike too many things!
It makes your life harder!

PERSUADE THEM!

Objective: Argue a point of view and try to persuade others to support it.

Activities Covered

- Choosing more persuasive statements
- Writing persuasive sentences
- **Group Work –** trying to persuade group of a given viewpoint

Background Information

This lesson focuses on students stating their point of view and trying to convince others to support the same view. Students must realize that being persuasive does not necessarily mean being argumentative; one can put a view across in a convincing and calm manner.

Before the Lesson

The teacher can have ready ideas as to when we need persuasive language.

The class will be divided into groups of six (maximum), and each member of the group will be given a different statement.

The Lesson (Pages 101 and 102)

The teacher can discuss persuasion with the class. When do we need to be persuasive? (Asking for something, convincing a friend to start football training with you, trying to convince parents you need to go to the concert, trying to convince the teacher not to give homework, etc.) It can be pointed out here that being persuasive is not the same as being argumentative. Results will be better if the students stay calm and are convincing in the words they choose. The teacher might also briefly mention how to stand your ground when someone is trying to persuade you to do something you don't want to do.

Students choose which one of two statements is more persuasive.

Students use persuasive language to convince someone that school is not that bad.

Students discuss their answers for Questions 1 and 2 with the class.

Group Work – Each member of the group receives a different statement from the teacher. Students think about how they will argue their point of view, writing short notes as prompts.

The group votes and students see if they have been successful or not.

Answers

1. (a) second statement
   (b) first statement
   (c) second statement
2.–3. Answers will vary, but possible persuasive sentences include:
   You would get bored all day at home because you would run out of things to do./ You would not be able to read or write properly, and then would not be able to find a good job./School is a place where you can make new friends./ School gives you the opportunity to speak to other students and adults./School teaches you about the world around you.
4. Possible statements:
   Proper school uniform must be worn to school.
   Students should only be allowed to bring healthy food to school. Chips, chocolates and sodas should be banned.
   Homework should be given every day, including Friday. If homework is not done, students should be fined.
   Students should do one hour of physical activity at school every day.
   There should be absolutely no talking in the classroom unless it is discussion time.
   No jewelry, apart from watches, should be worn to school.
5.–6. Teacher check

Additional Activities

Students can argue ridiculous or outrageous points of view; for example: Robots should be used to teach children/Children should be allowed to live in their own houses/Television should be banned for children under 12.

Persuade Them!

Sometimes we need to be persuasive in order to get what we want.

For example, sometimes you may have to persuade your parents to buy a particular present, or you may have to persuade a friend to go somewhere with you.

To persuade someone means to get them to believe you or agree with you.

1 Check which of these pairs of statements is more convincing.

(a)
☐ I like fried eggs because they are nice.

☐ I like fried eggs because I can have them crispy on the edges and soft in the middle.

(b)
☐ I want to go to the beach this summer because there is so much I enjoy doing there, like swimming, surfing, building sandcastles and collecting shells.

☐ I want to go to the beach this summer because I like to swim.

(c)
☐ I really need a new sweater because there is a dance coming up.

☐ I really would like a new sweater, as all my sweaters are old and worn and I look a bit too scruffy in them. They're also getting a bit tight!

2 Liam does not like school. (Isn't that strange?) How could you persuade him that it's not that bad? Write down a few things you could say to him.

_____

_____

_____

_____

_____

_____

_____

_____

3 Discuss your answers with your class.

Persuade Them!

④ Read the statement your teacher has given you.

Write it here.

_____

_____

_____

_____

_____

⑤ Think about how you could persuade the rest of your group to agree with your statement.

Write some things you could say here.

- _____

  _____

- _____

  _____

- _____

  _____

- _____

  _____

- _____

  _____

- _____

  _____

⑥ (a) Try to persuade your group. Use your notes to help you.

(b) How many votes did you get? ☐

A DAY IN THE LIFE

Objective: Explore historical events through improvisational drama.

Activities Covered

- Reading the diary extract
- Discussing the diary extract
- **Group Work –** acting out the scene based on the diary extract
- Presenting drama to the class
- Self-assessment

Background Information

The ancient Romans have been chosen for this lesson, but any historical event or time period can be used. Role-play is an excellent way to reinforce what has been learned in history.

Before the Lesson

The teacher can have additional information about Ancient Rome.

The class will be divided into groups.

The Lesson (Pages 103 and 104)

The teacher reads the given diary extract while the students follow.

The class has a discussion about this time period. The teacher can ask students questions. For example: How is Marco's life different from yours (toys, school life, breakfast, leisure activities)? Do you think Marco is rich or poor?

Group Work – Students act out a scene from this time. Each student must have a role.

Students can practice their scene in their groups several times before presenting it to the class.

Students assess their performance.

Answers

Teacher check

Additional Activities

Many history lessons can be reinforced with the use of improvisational drama.

Students can make up short stories for a particular time period and act them out.

A Day in the Life

1 Read a page of Marco's diary.

Marco lived in Ancient Rome. I think you will find his life very different from yours.

This morning, I got up early, before sunrise, to go to school. For breakfast I had some fruit, bread and fish. My slave cooked and cut my food for me, as we do not use knives and forks. We eat with our fingers or use spoons. I got dressed in my toga and made sure I had my bulla around my neck. A bulla is a special locket. It was given to me at my birth and I will wear it until I become a citizen, at the age of sixteen or seventeen.

I took a candle to school to use until daybreak. I walked past many beautiful buildings and temples. My slave walked with me, to make sure I got to school safely. At school we did writing on our board and used pebbles to do counting in math. We also learned how to write Roman numerals. I was good today and luckily did not get flogged with the whip! At lunchtime, we had a rest and an afternoon siesta and then it was time to go back to school. After school, my friends and I played board games and knucklebones. We also pretended we were having a war—we were all armed with wooden swords. My sister and her friends were playing with dolls!

We strolled through the city and there were many people about. Some were walking. Others were being carried in litters, curtained couches carried on poles by slaves. Soldiers were walking about in chain mail or leather armor, and workmen were wearing their tunics. Many shops lined the streets. There were also orators (speakers), and every now and then, someone stopped to listen to what they were saying and gave their views. In the evening, after dinner, my family and I went to the Colosseum, which is a huge public entertainment center that can seat 45,000 spectators! We watched the gladiators and humans fighting wild animals. It was quite gruesome! I enjoy going to the Circus Maximus, which is another center, but they have mostly chariot racing. It is a bigger place and can seat 250,000 people! Sometimes we go to the theater. Most events there are free.

A Day in the Life

My dad loves to going to the baths and goes there every day. Unfortunately, no students are allowed. There are warm baths and cold baths. The water for the warm baths is heated by fires under the floor. Slaves keep these fires going. Also at the baths are a reading room, a shop, a barber and sporting events.

I took time out to honor the gods, which is a part of everyday life. There are temples all over the Roman Empire, and each home has a household god.

Back at home, our family gathered in the atrium to discuss the evening's entertainment, but I was too tired and went to bed. Goodnight! Marco.

Did you know?

In Ancient Rome, dirt and rubbish were thrown out of the windows into the streets!

2 Work as a group to act out a scene based on Marco's diary. Make sure everyone has a role and something to say and do. Write a list of everyone's role here.

Name	Role

3 Perform your scene for your class.

4 (a) Give your performance a mark out of 5. ☐

(b) How could your performance be improved? _____

_____

_____

WHAT DO YOU THINK OF THIS?

Objective: Explore reactions to ideas through improvisational drama.

Activities Covered

- Answering questions about events in their local area
- Discussing answers with their class
- **Group Work** – role-playing things they can do with their friends
- Writing responses to ideas
- **Pair Work** – role-playing a scene

Background Information

In this lesson, specific ideas are given that the students must write about and role-play. Although only one particular scene has been used for role-play, all of the ideas can be incorporated into improvisational drama. There are many different scenarios that can be used, but they must be issues that directly affect the students and to which they will have a reaction of some sort.

Before the Lesson

The teacher can have a list of other scenarios that the students can role-play.

The class will be divided into pairs.

The Lesson (Pages 107 and 108)

Students discuss questions about events in their town/area with their partner.

Students answer questions about their leisure time and what they would like to have in the town in the way of entertainment.

Students discuss their answers with the class, and some students can role-play different activities that they and their friends could do if there were extra attractions.

Students write responses for the given statements and answer the questions.

Students discuss all the answers with the class.

Pair Work – Students role-play a given situation. (Others can be added.)

Answers

1.–5.   Teacher check.

Additional Activities

Students can come up with their own ideas on a particular theme and then can role-play those ideas; for example, things to do at break time, how they would like to be treated.

What Do You Think of This?

1 Discuss and answer these questions with your partner.

(a) What events are going on in your town/area at the moment?

_____

_____

_____

_____

(b) Are there any events you will attend? Which events?

_____

_____

(c) What kind of entertainment would you like to see in your town/area?

_____

_____

_____

_____

(d) Name some activities you do on the weekend.

_____

_____

_____

_____

(e) What could you do to stop yourself from getting bored?

_____

_____

_____

_____

2 Discuss your answers with the class.

3 With your partner, role-play activities that you could do with a friend.

What Do You Think of This?

4 Discuss and write what you think of these ideas with your partner.

(a)

Students in elementary school should be allowed to choose which subjects they are taught.

(b)

Students should be able to leave the school grounds at break and lunchtime.

(c)

There should be "CHILDREN ONLY" stores that only sell all the things that children like. No adults should be allowed to enter.

5 Work with your partner to role-play the manager of the shop telling your parents they are not allowed in!

BOOK PARTS

Objective: Know the structure and terminology of books.

Activities Covered

- Finding out the meanings of terms
- Describing terms to class
- Listening to terms described by others and writing notes

Background Information

This lesson focuses on the different terms used when talking about books. The definitions are decided as a class and all the terms are further reinforced when students talk about the term they have been given.

Before the Lesson

Students will need time to research their word; perhaps the term can be given for homework.

The classroom should have a collection of many different types of books that students can use to demonstrate their term if they are unable to bring one from home.

The Lesson (Pages 110 and 111)

The teacher must read through the terms with the students.

Students are each given a specific term. The teacher can do the extra ones if there are words left over. If there are more than 30 students in your class, students can double on a word.

Students describe the term to the class, demonstrating its meaning, if possible.

The class discusses the word and students write in a suitable definition.

Answers

1. Chapter – Division of a book
2. Page – One side of a sheet of paper forming a book
3. Index – Alphabetical list of names or subjects dealt with in a book, file, or catalog; used to find information
4. Author – Writer of a book
5. Title – Name of a book, film, etc.
6. Illustration – Picture
7. Cover – Anything that covers the outside of a book, magazine
8. Publisher – One who prints books
9. ISBN number – Book number, found at front and back of a book
10. Comic – Magazine containing cartoon strips
11. Magazine – Periodical publication with articles by different writers, television or radio programs made up of short, nonfictional items
12. Introduction – Preliminary part of the book
13. Table of contents – List of what is in the book
14. Spine – Edge of a book on which the title is written
15. Hardback – Book that has a hard cover
16. Paperback – Book that has a "soft" cover made from thin cardboard
17. Review – Critical assessment of a book
18. Fiction – Invented story
19. Nonfiction – Fact
20. Caption – Title or explanation accompanying an illustration
21. Price – What the book costs
22. Copyright – Exclusive legal right to reproduce and control a book
23. Autobiography – Account of a person's life written by the person
24. Biography – Account of a person's life written by another person
25. Editor – Person who edits; person in charge of a newspaper/magazine
26. Novel – Long, fictitious story in book form
27. Librarian – One who works in a library
28. Text – The main body of a book, as distinct from illustrations
29. Illustrator – One who illustrates
30. Publication date – The date the book was published

Additional Activities

The students can create a classroom display with different types of books, and some of the terms learned in the lesson can be used to label their displays.

Students should be encouraged to use some terms when doing their next book review.

Book Parts

Each student will receive a term to explain to the class.

What was your word?

_____

We are going to learn about different parts of a book.
It's not just words, you know!

Write the meanings of the terms below as each student gives his/her description.

Term	Description
(1) Chapter	
(2) Page	
(3) Index	
(4) Author	
(5) Title	
(6) Illustration	
(7) Cover	
(8) Publisher	
(9) ISBN number	
(10) Comic	
(11) Magazine	
(12) Introduction	
(13) Table of contents	

Book Parts

Term	Description
(14) Spine	
(15) Hardback	
(16) Paperback	
(17) Review	
(18) Fiction	
(19) Nonfiction	
(20) Caption	
(21) Price	
(22) Copyright	
(23) Autobiography	
(24) Biography	
(25) Editor	
(26) Novel	
(27) Librarian	
(28) Text	
(29) Illustrator	
(30) Publication date	

CAN YOU REMEMBER?

Objective: Describe everyday experiences to the class or group and discuss them.

Activities Covered

- Answering questions about their morning
- **Group work –** students tell the group about their morning
- **Pair work –** students write, ask and answer questions about yesterday

Background Information

In this lesson, students learn to talk about general everyday things. Hopefully, they will have some fun recalling the details of their morning. Students should get practice in "just chatting" – the teacher could give time for conversation. It is an important part of communicating!

Before the Lesson

The class will be divided into groups and then pairs.

The Lesson (Pages 113 and 114)

Students answer questions about their morning.

Group Work – Students tell the group about their morning. The teacher needs to explain to students that not all the questions need to be given to the group; their talk should be "off the cuff." The questions are there to jog students' memories!

Pair Work – Students write five questions they could ask their partner about yesterday. Students ask their partner the questions, listening carefully and noting the answers.

Students use their partner's answers to describe their partner's day.

Answers

Teacher check

Additional Activities

Students can tell the group about their weekend/last meal/a trip/their day at school (ordinary everyday experiences).

Can You Remember?

1) Answer these questions about this morning.

(a) What did you have to eat for breakfast this morning?

_____

_____

(b) What did you have to drink?

_____

_____

(c) What time did you get up?

_____

_____

(d) Whom did you see before you came to school?

_____

_____

(e) What was the weather like when you woke up?

_____

_____

(f) Which did you do first?
   get dressed/brush teeth/ have breakfast/other

_____

_____

(g) Where were your shoes?

_____

_____

(h) Who was the first person you saw when you arrived at school?

_____

_____

(i) How did you feel this morning?

_____

_____

(j) Name something you saw on your way to school.

_____

_____

(k) What was the last thing you did just before you left your home?

_____

_____

(l) What color socks did you put on this morning?

_____

_____

2) Were you able to answer all of the questions? _____

3) Take turns to describe your morning to your group.

Do you think your morning sounded interesting? [yes] [no]

Did you know?
am stands for ante meridiem (before noon)

Can You Remember?

4 Write five questions to ask your partner about what he/she did yesterday.

My Questions

(a) _____

_____

(b) _____

_____

(c) _____

_____

(d) _____

_____

(e) _____

_____

5 Listen carefully to your partner's answers and write them here.

My Partner's Answers

My partner is _____ .

(a) _____

_____

(b) _____

_____

(c) _____

_____

(d) _____

_____

(e) _____

_____

6 Use your partner's answers to describe his or her day.

THE BEST BIT

Objective: Discuss favorite moments, important events and exciting characters in a book or movie.

Activities Covered

- Recalling favorite moments
- Answering questions about a movie or book
- Discussing all answers with the class

Background Information

Discussion should be the main focus of the lesson, allowing students to give more depth to their thoughts on what they have read, experienced and seen. Students should be encouraged to think about characters in the movies and programs they see and the books they read.

Before the Lesson

The teacher could have an example for the students; for example, they can think of their last birthday/vacation/any special event and describe their favorite moments to the class; describe the people who were present at the time.

The Lesson (Pages 116 and 117)

Students answer questions, recalling particular events and what their best moments were.

Students think about a movie they have seen or a book they have read and answer questions about it.

Students share their answers with the rest of the class.

Answers

Teacher check

Additional Activities

The same type of lesson can be done with poetry, where characters are discussed and the students state their favorite parts of the poem. This would work well with humorous poetry.

Plays could also be read for this purpose.

Students can have a discussion about their favorite moments at school and write a paragraph about them.

The Best Bit

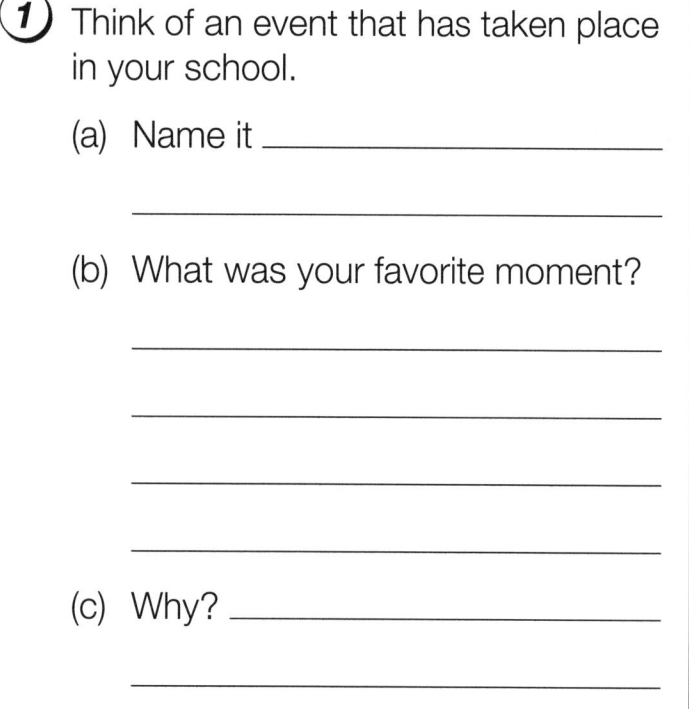

My favorite moment was when I won the tennis match.

1 Think of an event that has taken place in your school.

(a) Name it _____

_____

(b) What was your favorite moment?

_____

_____

_____

_____

(c) Why? _____

_____

_____

2 Think of a place that you have visited.

(a) Name it _____

_____

_____

_____

(b) What was your favorite moment there?

_____

_____

_____

_____

_____

_____

_____

_____

(c) Why? _____

_____

_____

_____

3 Think of a celebration that you have had.

(a) Name it _____

_____

(b) What was your favorite moment?

_____

_____

_____

_____

(c) Why? _____

_____

_____

4 (a) Discuss your answers with your class.

(b) Did anyone have the same favorite moment as you? _____

The Best Bit

(5) Think about a movie you have watched or a book you have read.

Answer these questions.

(a) What is the title of the movie or book? _____

(b) What was your favorite part? _____

_____

_____

_____

(c) Which character did you like the best and why? _____

_____

_____

(d) Name an important event in the movie or book. _____

_____

_____

_____

(e) Sum up the movie or book in one word. _____

(f) Draw three scenes from this movie or book.

(g) Discuss all your answers with your class.

WHO STARS IN YOUR STORIES?

Objective: Express reactions to events and characters in stories.
Objective: Discuss reactions to poems.

Activities Covered

- Reading a story as a group
- **Group Work –** answering questions
- Discussing story
- Describing a character from a story

Background Information

This lesson uses a fairy tale as the reading because the story will be familiar to the whole class. The lesson should get students to think about the plot and characters in the story. This can also be done with the class reader. Students should be encouraged to question what they read and think about different components of the story. Two objectives have been included as the same type of lesson can be done with a poem.

Before the Lesson

The teacher can use a poem as an example, asking the students questions about the events and characters in a poem. Answers to questions should not be obvious; students will need to do a little thinking!

The class will be divided into groups.

The Lesson (Pages 119 and 120)

Group Work – Students read the story of *Little Red Riding Hood*.

Students answer questions.

Students discuss their answers and the story.

Students describe to the group a character in one of their favorite stories.

If there is time, each group can discuss their answers with the class.

Answers

1. Teacher check
2. Answers will vary, but could include:
   (a) any age under 12
   (b) It was a special cape that had been made for her by her grandmother./She lived in a cold place./It was her favorite item of clothing.
   (c) She was packing her picnic basket./She had been to school.
   (d) She was kind and considerate, but a little daring. Her mom was always telling her to be careful.
   (e) Any suitable name
   (f) Grandma was kind, but sometimes a little grumpy.
   (g) It was a 10-minute walk through the woods, but it took 20 minutes because she dawdled.
   (h) The wolf was sly and cunning and was not to be trusted.
   (i) She may have become far more careful about walking around on her own, and I don't think she ever went through the woods again.
   (j) No, I don't think the wolf should have been harmed.
   (k) I would change the ending. I think the wolf should have been arrested and thrown in jail!
   (l) Teacher check
3. Teacher check

Additional Activities

Poems can be used for students to discuss events and characters, looking beyond what may have been written in the poem.

Students can watch a popular movie and answer the same sort of questions, the answers requiring them to consider something based on what they have seen; for example, describing characters, etc.

Who Stars in Your Stories?

1 Read the story of **Little Red Riding Hood** with your group.

You may have read it before, but it was probably a long time ago!

2 Answer these questions. Use your imagination!

(a) How old do you think Little Red Riding Hood was? _____

(b) Why did she wear the cape? _____

_____

_____

(c) What do you think she was doing before she went to Grandma's house?

_____

_____

(d) What do you think she was like? _____

_____

_____

(e) What could her real name have been? (Have a group vote for the name that suits her best.)

_____

_____

(f) What do you think Grandma was like? _____

_____

_____

(g) How long do you think it took her to get to Grandma's house? Why?

_____

_____

(h) What type of character did the wolf have? _____

_____

_____

Who Stars in Your Stories?

(i) How do you think the event would have changed her life? _____

_____

_____

(j) Do you think the story ended well? Say why. _____

_____

(k) What part of the story would you change? _____

_____

_____

(l) Give the story a score out of 10. ☐

③ (a) What is your all-time favorite fairy tale?

_____

Did you know?
Charles Perrault was the author of **Little Red Riding Hood.**

(b) You are going to describe one of the characters from this story to your group. Write some notes to help you.

My character is _____

(c) Describe the character to your group.

TELL YOUR STORY

Objective: Create and tell stories to the class or group and retell them after questioning, comparing the versions.

Activities Covered

- Thinking of a story
- Writing keywords
- Telling a story
- Making up answers to questions from the group
- Writing a story
- Comparing versions, stating two differences

Background Information

This lesson may take some time, as students are writing and telling their stories. Students must be given sufficient time to think of their story. The lesson is about students thinking of a story, telling their story and, after questions have been asked by the group, students writing their story. Thus, the second version of their story should not be the same, and this should be mentioned to the students. The questions that have been asked by the group should prompt students to think of other ideas for their story, which should be included in the written version. It is important that students compare the two versions and notice the differences.

Before the Lesson

The class will be divided into groups.

The Lesson (Pages 122 and 123)

Students think of a story, using a beginning which has been given to them.

Students write down keywords to help them remember their story. (Students must write only keywords and not sentences.)

Group Work – Students tell their story to the group.

The group must ask questions about the story and the storyteller should make up the answers.

After all the students have told their story, students write their story.

Students compare the two versions of their story and write down two differences.

Answers

Teacher check

Additional Activities

The same lesson can be done where a specific topic is chosen. The students must, for this lesson, be writing fictional material.

Tell Your Story

You are going to tell a story to your group.

Keep your story quite short, but make it interesting!

1 Think of your story and write down keywords in the box to help you remember how your story goes.

This is how the story starts:

Once upon a time, there was a spoiled boy called Kevin. Everything he wanted, he got. There was nothing in the world his parents wouldn't buy him. His room was stuffed with toys and games, but he always wanted more.

2 Tell your story to your group. You can glance at your keywords to remind you.

3 When you have finished, your group will ask you questions about your story. You can make up the answers as you go.

Tell Your Story

4 Write your story. It doesn't have to be exactly the same as the story you told the group—try to make it even better!

_____

_____

_____

_____

_____

_____

_____

_____

_____

_____

_____

_____

_____

_____

_____

_____

5 Write two differences between the story you told the group and the story you wrote.

(a) _____

_____

(b) _____

_____

6 Do you think your story got better? [yes] [no]

HAVE SOME FEELINGS!

Objective: Express feelings and attitudes through improvisational drama.

Activities Covered

- Describing feelings
- Acting out scenes with feelings
- Writing conversation
- Acting out a family scene
- Discussing scenes

Background Information

This lesson is about students expressing their feelings through role-play. The scenes acted out should be familiar situations for the students. The acting should be extemporized.

Before the Lesson

The class will be divided into pairs and groups of four or five.

The Lesson (Pages 125 and 126)

Pair work – Students write how they would feel in different situations.

Students act out the same scenes. (Teacher can explain to students that these need only be short scenes, as they have a few to get through!)

Students write down a possible conversation (family dinner).

Students act out a family dinner scene, in small groups.

Answers

1. Answers will vary, but could include:
   (a) confused, nervous, worried
   (b) happy, excited
   (c) angry, disappointed
   (d) sick, unhappy
   (e) excited
   (f) embarrassed, ashamed, hurt
   (g) proud, happy
   (h) nervous, shy
   (i) disappointed, angry, helpless
   (j) ashamed, sad, worried
2. Teacher check
3. Answers will vary, but a possible conversation is:
   Dad: I did not have a great day. How was everybody else's day?
   Mom: Not that wonderful, either. I am almost sure I saw a mouse running through the kitchen.
   John: I got into trouble at school today because I fell asleep in class.
   Sally: I had a wonderful day because I got top marks for my history test.
   David: My day was OK, except Mickey isn't in his cage and I can't seem to find him.
4.–6. Teacher check

Additional Activities

Students can act out scenes from school.

Have Some Feelings!

1 Work with your partner to write how you might feel in the following situations.

How do you feel when ...

(a) you don't understand something in class?

_____

_____

Weekends make me happy!

(b) your best friend invites you to stay for the weekend?

_____

_____

(c) someone breaks something precious of yours?

_____

_____

(d) you have to eat food you really don't like?

_____

_____

(e) vacation is just a day away?

_____

_____

(f) the teacher shouts at you?

_____

_____

(g) you get excellent marks in a test?

_____

_____

(h) you have to stand up in front of the class and give a talk?

_____

_____

(i) your parents don't allow you to do something?

_____

_____

(j) you've been nasty to someone you are close to?

_____

_____

2 Work with your partner to act out a scene for each of the situations above. Make it up as you go!

Have Some Feelings!

3) *Imagine a family all sitting down to dinner. There's Dad, Mom, the teenage son, John, the 10–year old sister, Sally, and the little brother, David, who is just six.*

Work with your partner to write what they might say.

Dad: _____

_____

Mom: _____

_____

John: _____

_____

Sally: _____

_____

David: _____

_____

4) Go around the class, with each pair giving their sentence for whichever person is next. It should make a strange conversation!

5) (a) Work in small groups to act out a family dinner.

(b) Perform your act for your class.

(c) Discuss the different acts.

6) Write words that describe your family dinners.

IN THE FUTURE

Objective: Create and sustain imaginary contexts through improvisational drama.

Activities Covered

- **Group Work** – writing words
- Acting out a scene
- Adding more words to a list
- Writing an imagined description
- Reading descriptions to the class
- Discussing the topic with the class

Background Information

In this lesson, students must act out a scene, and then discussion about the theme must take place, based on the acting students have seen. After the discussion, students could write various pieces on the topic, such as a diary for a day in space, my futuristic school/family/pet, etc.

Before the Lesson

The teacher could tell students about the first space tourist, Mark Shuttleworth, and students could think about other possible futuristic vacations.

The class will be divided into groups.

The Lesson (Pages 128 and 129)

Group Work – Students get given a time limit to discuss what the year 3000 may be like, and they must write appropriate words in the box.

Students discuss acting out a scene from this time, with each person in the group getting a part to play.

Time must be given for students to practice the scene a few times. (Performances do not need to be perfect and can be mostly made up as they go.)

Students watch the other groups present their performances and add words to their futuristic word list.

Students write briefly about what the world will be like (individual).

Students discuss their ideas and the acted scenes with the class.

Answers

Answers will vary. Possible futuristic words:

robots, space shuttles, self-cleaning houses, flying automobiles, virtual shopping, drive-through banks, cyberpets, computerized bicycles, virtual books, interactive TVs, students being taught by computers, voice-activated pens, cures for diseases, movie-sized TVs, etc.

Additional Activities

Any theme can be chosen for this type of lesson, where students act out imaginary scenes; for example, a topic from history.

In the Future

It is the year 3000! How different will the world be?

1 How many years from now is the year 3000? ☐

2 (a) Work as a group to write what you think the world will be like in the year 3000.

You only need to write words, not sentences, and you can make up as many things as you like!

(b) How many words did you write? ☐

3 Work with your group to create a scene from this time. Decide where your scene takes place. It could be at school, at home, in a store, or anywhere! You can make up objects and places too!

4 Act your scene out for the class.

What will the teachers be like in the future?

5 (a) After watching each group perform its scene, add more "futuristic" words to your box.

(b) How many extra words did you write? ☐

In the Future

6 Write what you think the world will be like in the year 3000. Add a picture.

_____

_____

_____

_____

_____

_____

_____

_____

_____

_____

_____

_____

_____

_____

_____

_____

_____

7 Read your description to your class or group and explain your picture.

Did you know?
It is thought that the first space tourist, Mark Shuttleworth, paid $20 million to visit space. That's quite an expensive vacation!

POETRY TIME

Objective: React to poems through improvisational drama.
Objective: Dramatize stories.

Activities Covered

- Reading aloud as a class
- **Group Work –** acting out a poem
- Performing for the class
- Assessing performance
- Drawing a picture and telling the group about it

Background Information

This lesson is not just acting out a poem, but also acting out the student's interpretations of the poem. The teacher should tell students that although they need to follow the actions stated in the poem, they can add their own twists to them. Dramatizing stories should also be done, and virtually any type of story can be used, provided they are not too long. Students are not expected to give polished performances; the acting should be more casual and ad-lib. Before any dramatization takes place, it is important that it is preceded with discussion on the plot, characters, events, etc.

Before the Lesson

The teacher could have other poems available for students to act out so that groups are doing different poems (optional).

The class will be divided into groups.

The Lesson (Pages 131 and 132)

The class will read the given poem out loud and together.

The class must discuss the poem; what type of characters they think they are, setting, etc.

Group Work – Students assign roles to each other and write these down.

Students practice their performance a few times.

Students perform their poem for the class.

Students assess their performance.

Students draw a picture and tell their group about it.

Answers

Teacher check

Additional Activities

Students can bring their favorite poems to class and act them out in groups.

Students can dramatize a story that is well known to them; for example, a fairy tale, a class reader.

Poetry Time

(1) Read this poem together as a class.

Sunshine

Rain had fallen for days and days,
and then the sun came through.

Dad said, "Go and get the steak;
we'll have a barbecue."
Mom said, "Great, I'll hang out the clothes;
I'll have dry washing at last."
Josh said, "I'm going to ride my bike;
watch me go right past."
Jason said, "I'll be on my skateboard;
I can practice my new trick."
"I'm off to visit a friend," said James.
"Being indoors makes me sick!"
The cat said, "I'm off to frighten birds;
don't wait up for me."
I went outside to soak up the heat;
the warmth was healing me.

Yes, what an enormous difference
the sun made to our day.
The house it fell quite silent
as we all went out to play.

(2) Discuss the following with your class.

(a) What type of character is each person in the poem?

(b) Where is the poem set?

(c) When is the poem set?

(d) Whether you like this poem or not and why.

(e) What you would do after several days of rain.

Poetry Time

3 Work with your group to act out this poem.

(a) Write the names of the students in your group and their role.

Name of Student	Role

(b) How did your group perform?

very well   well   quite well

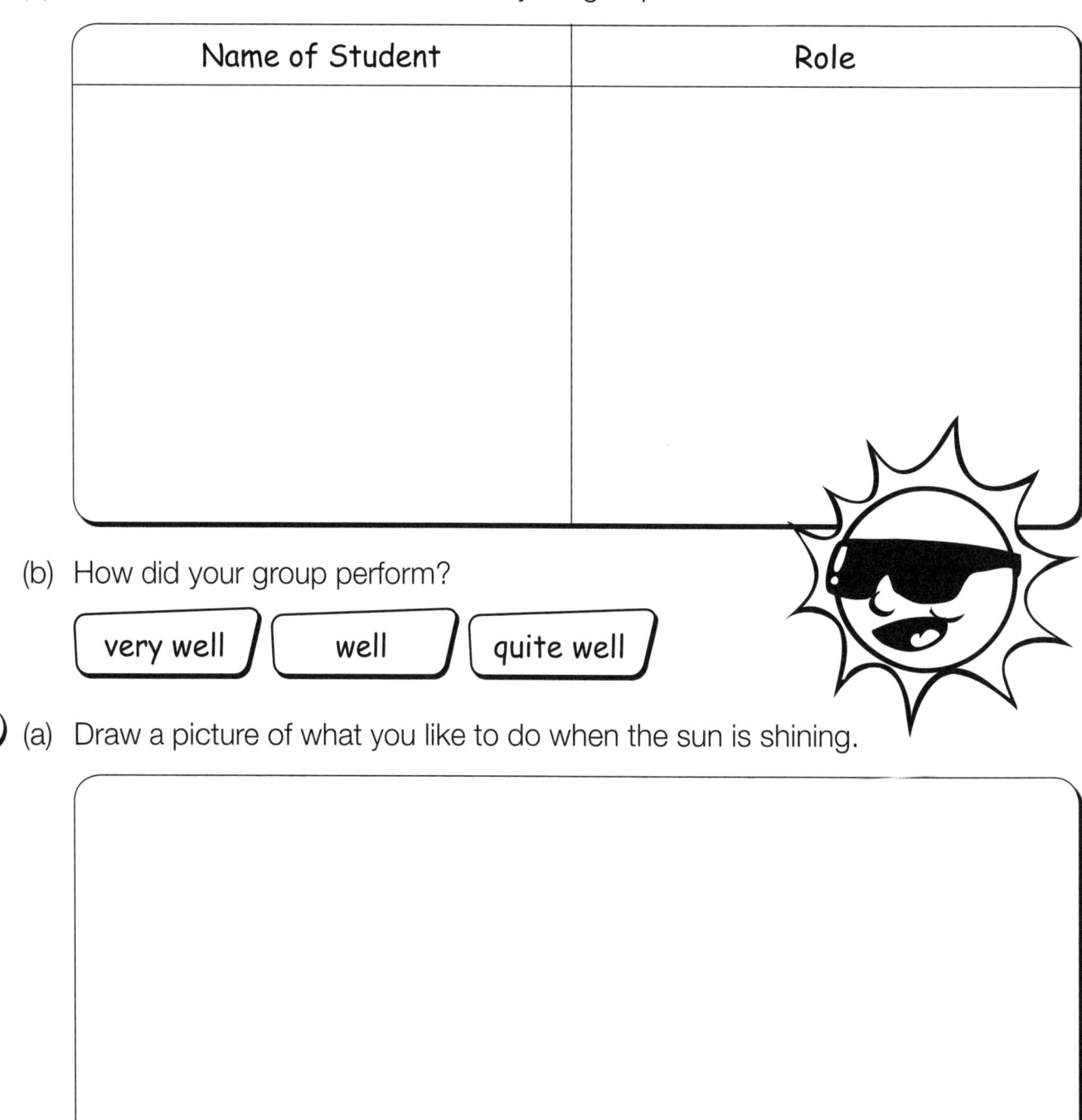

4 (a) Draw a picture of what you like to do when the sun is shining.

(b) Show your picture to your group. Tell them what you like doing when the sun is shining.

FUN WITH WORDS

Objective: Experience and enjoy playful aspects of language.

Activities Covered

- Listening to teacher using challenging words
- Guessing meanings
- **Group Work –** looking up true meanings
- Completing and writing sentences

Background Information

This lesson deals with funny and unusual words, but there is no end to having fun in language lessons. Students love telling jokes and playing games, so include these types of lessons often to keep up interest.

Before the Lesson

The teacher can have a list of unusual words to discuss with the students.

The class will be divided into groups.

Dictionaries will be needed.

The Lesson (Pages 134 and 135)

Students say the words out loud. The teacher can help with the pronunciation by telling students to break the words up into syllables.

The teacher reads the sentences that contain the words.

Students guess the meanings of the words.

Group Work – The teacher reads the sentences again.

Students discuss their guesses, one by one, with their group.

The group looks up the true meanings of the words in the dictionary.

Students discuss and complete the sentences in their group.

Groups write sentences, using challenging words provided.

All words can then be discussed as a class.

Answers

1.–3.
   Possible sentences containing list of words (for the teacher to use), including meanings:
   (a) It is good manners to **doff** your hat when you greet someone. *(lift, take off)*
   (b) The dog is so **scraggy**, it looks as if it has not been fed in ages. *(thin and bony)*
   (c) I can't understand you when you speak such **gobbledegook**. *(unintelligible language, jargon)*
   (d) It's a relief we don't have to wear **knickerbockers** to school nowadays, as I hate showing off my legs. *(loose-fitting short trousers gathered in at the knee)*
   (e) I threw the ingredients into the bowl **willy-nilly** when I made my Christmas cake, and it flopped. *(in a haphazard way)*
   (f) My teacher likes to **flummox** me with the most difficult questions in math. *(puzzle)*
   (g) My uncle is always playing the fool and acting like a **twit**. *(foolish person)*
   (h) I think it's **poppycock** that your dog ate your homework for breakfast! *(nonsense, rubbish)*
   (i) My mother always makes such a **kerfuffle** about my clothes when we go out. *(fuss)*
   (j) It is a load of **codswallop** that we have to do three hours of homework every day! *(nonsense, rubbish)*
   (k) I don't know where your project begins or where it ends—it is **higgledy-piggledy**. *(in confusion or disorder)*
   (l) My friend always gets into trouble for talking in class—she is such a **flibbertigibbet**. *(talkative or flighty person)*
4. (a) flibbertigibbet (b) codswallop
   (c) higgledy-piggledy (d) kerfuffle
5.–6. Teacher check

Additional Activities

Students can use these words in oral sentences.

The class could have a joke-telling lesson.

The class could play word-association games.

Students could read and listen to humorous literature.

Students could make up funny rhymes and verses, using strange and unusual words.

Fun with Words

1 Listen to the teacher use the words in sentences.

We are going to look at some strange words. Say these words aloud.

Word	Your Guess	True Meaning
(a) doff		
(b) scraggy		
(c) gobbledegook		
(d) knickerbockers		
(e) willy-nilly		
(f) flummox		
(g) twit		
(h) poppycock		
(i) kerfuffle		
(j) codswallop		
(k) higgledy-piggledy		
(l) flibbertigibbet		

2 After your teacher reads each sentence, write what you think each word means in the "Your Guess" column of the table.

Try some of these words out on your family. I think they'll be impressed!

3 Work as a group to look up the words in your dictionary to see if your guess was correct!

How many words did you guess correctly?

Fun with Words

④ Work with your group. Choose words from the box below to complete these sentences.

(a) My aunt's telephone bill must be very high as she is such a

_____ .

(b) My brother says that he saw an alien, but he always speaks such

_____ no one believes him.

(c) The clothes in your wardrobe are so _____
I don't know how you manage to find anything.

(d) I wish my grandmother wouldn't make such a _____
about me eating my vegetables.

| codswallop | higgledy-piggledy | kerfuffle | flibbertigibbet |

⑤ Work with your group. Write sentences to include these words.

(a) poppycock

_____

_____

(b) willy-nilly

_____

_____

(c) gobbledegook

_____

_____

(d) flummox

_____

_____

(e) scraggy

_____

_____

⑥ Discuss your answers to Questions 4 and 5 with the class.